THE *Passion* BOOK

BUDDHISM AND MODERNITY

A series edited by Donald S. Lopez Jr.

Recent Books in the Series

A Storied Sage (2016), by Micah L. Auerback

Strange Tales of an Oriental Idol (2016), by Donald S. Lopez Jr.

Rescued from the Nation (2015), by Steven Kemper

Grains of Gold (2013), by Gendun Chopel

The Birth of Insight (2013), by Erik Braun

Religious Bodies Politic (2013), by Anya Bernstein

THE *Passion* BOOK

A TIBETAN GUIDE TO LOVE & SEX

Gendun Chopel

TRANSLATED AND WITH AN AFTERWORD
BY DONALD S. LOPEZ JR. AND THUPTEN JINPA

THE UNIVERSITY OF CHICAGO PRESS • CHICAGO AND LONDON

The University of Chicago Press, Chicago 60637
The University of Chicago Press, Ltd., London

Published 2018
Printed in the United States of America

27 26 25 24 23 22 21 20 19 18 1 2 3 4 5

ISBN-13: 978-0-226-52003-2 (cloth)
ISBN-13: 978-0-226-52017-9 (paper)
ISBN-13: 978-0-226-52020-9 (e-book)
DOI: https://doi.org/10.7208/chicago/9780226520209.001.0001

The University of Chicago Press gratefully acknowledges the generous support of the University of Michigan toward the publication of this book.

Library of Congress Cataloging-in-Publication Data

Names: Dge-'dun-chos-'phel, A-mdo, 1903–1951, author. | Lopez, Donald S., Jr., 1952– translator, writer of postface. | Thupten Jinpa, translator, writer of postface.
Title: The passion book : a Tibetan guide to love & sex / Gendun Chopel ; translated and with an afterword by Donald S. Lopez Jr. and Thupten Jinpa.
Other titles: 'Dod pa'i bstan bcos. English. 2018 | Buddhism and modernity.
Description: Chicago ; London : The University of Chicago Press, 2018. |
Series: Buddhism and modernity | Includes bibliographical references
Identifiers: LCCN 2017024328 | ISBN 9780226520032 (cloth : alk. paper) | ISBN 9780226520179 (pbk. : alk. paper) | ISBN 9780226520209 (e-book)
Subjects: LCSH: Sex instruction—Religious aspects—Buddhism—Poetry. | Sex—Religious aspects—Buddhism—Poetry. | LCGFT: Poetry.
Classification: LCC PL3748.D4 D613 2018 | DDC 306.7—dc23
LC record available at https://lccn.loc.gov/2017024328

♾ This paper meets the requirements of ANSI/NISO Z39.48-1992 (Permanence of Paper).

Contents

AFTERWORD: BACKGROUND TO *A TREATISE ON PASSION*

*

PREFACE

A Treatise on Passion is the most famous, and infamous, work of Gendun Chopel, the most important, and controversial, Tibetan writer of the twentieth century. He was born in the far northeast region of the Tibetan cultural domain in 1903, the year that British forces under the command of Colonel Francis Younghusband invaded his homeland. He died in 1951, as troops of the Peoples Liberation Army marched through the streets of Lhasa. Over the course of his short life, he was identified as an incarnate lama, ordained as a Buddhist monk, excelled on the debating courtyards of Tibet's great monasteries, and left Tibet for India, not returning again for twelve years. There, he gave up his monk's vows, learned to paint in a style unknown in Tibet, learned Sanskrit, and wrote some of the greatest Tibetan poetry of the twentieth century. Returning to his native land in 1945, he was arrested on trumped-up charges of treason and thrown into prison. Emerging a broken man, he lived long enough to compose a controversial treatise on Buddhist philosophy, one that continues to provoke heated arguments to this day.

Among all of his writings—the many that survive and the many that are lost—none is more famous than his *Treatise on Passion*. His motivations for writing the text were many. The first was largely academic. Like so many Tibetan intellectuals, he had a fascination with classical Indian literary culture. Upon his arrival in India, he found a genre of classical literature that was not well known in Tibet. This is *kāmaśāstra*, works on erotica, the most famous (but certainly not the only) example of which is the *Kāma Sūtra*. Gendun Chopel studied many works of Sanskrit erotica as he prepared to write his own text in Tibetan. Readers of the *Kāma Sūtra* are often surprised (and disappointed) to learn that only a few of its chapters deal with sex. It is less a sex manual and more a guidebook for the proper conduct of the cultured Indian gentleman in his dealings with women. Gendun Chopel, who was both an admirer and a critic of classical Indian culture, dispenses with most of this. His interest is sexual pleasure.

This is a pleasure that he knew not from books but from his own experience. And thus his second motivation in composing his *Treatise on Passion* was to convey that experience. In poem after poem, on page after page, we find the exuberance of someone discovering the joys of sex, made all the more intense because they had been forbidden to him for so long. He had taken vows of celibacy when he was in his early teens and may have renounced his monk's vows as late as age thirty-one, just four years before completing this work, where he describes in ecstatic and graphic detail the wonders he had discovered. These are among the most powerful passages in the work and are the places where we hear Gendun Chopel's voice most clearly, a voice with tints of irony, self-deprecating wit, and a love of women, not merely as sources of male pleasure, but as full partners in the play of passion.

However, Gendun Chopel had yet another motivation. As an incarnate lama of the "ancient" sect of Tibetan Buddhism, he was deeply versed in the tantras, those texts that set forth secret techniques for achieving enlightenment, techniques that result in deep states of bodily bliss, bliss that becomes Buddhahood. In some tantric systems, in order to achieve enlightenment, the subtle mind of bliss must penetrate the profound nature of reality. Gendun Chopel was a learned tantric exegete, having studied with great masters in Tibet. Here, in *A Treatise on Passion*, he seeks to understand the meaning of bliss and how it relates to the pleasures of lovemaking.

Gendun Chopel arrived in India during the height of the independence movement, as Hindu and Muslim patriots sought to throw off the colonial chains of British bondage. He was deeply sympathetic to this movement, taking many of its principles back to Tibet with him. Yet Gendun Chopel would become an apostle of a different freedom: sexual freedom. He condemned the hypocrisy of society and church, instead portraying sexual pleasure as a force of nature and a human right for all. The *kāmaśāstra* literature of India was intended for the socially elite; the tantric literature of Tibet was intended for the spiritually advanced. And whether intended for the cultured gentleman or the tantric yogin, the instructions were provided for men. In his *Treatise on Passion*, Gendun Chopel seeks to wrest the erotic from the elite and give it to the people, of all genders. These are among the most powerful passages in the work and are the places where we again recognize Gendun Chopel's voice. As you will read in the pages that follow:

74. Not spitefully binding or beating someone,
Not cruelly stabbing someone with a spear;
Passion is offered to a passionate human.
It may not be a virtue, but how could it be a sin?

298. This passion that arises so naturally
In all men and women without effort

Is covered by a thin veil of shame.
With just a little effort, it shows its true face, naked.

588. May all humble people who live on this broad earth
Be delivered from the pit of merciless laws
And be able to indulge, with freedom,
In common enjoyments, so needed and right.

A TREATISE ON PASSION

One

THE SEXUAL PRACTICES OF WOMEN OF VARIOUS LANDS

In the language of India, *Kāmaśāstra*. In the language of Tibet, *A Treatise on Passion*.

Homage to the Buddha.

1. May you be protected by self-arisen Mahāmudrā.[1]
Its lightning lasso of immutable vajra bliss,
Reaching to the bounds of the eight and eight,[2]
Binds the still and moving into one reality.

1. The Sanskrit term *mahāmudrā*, often translated as "great seal," is of particular importance in tantric Buddhism. In this verse, it refers to a luminous and blissful realization of the ultimate nature of reality. Such a state is generally achieved through advanced tantric practices for controlling the subtle energies in the body. Here, however, it is called "self-arisen," implying that the realization arises naturally and spontaneously.

2. If "eight and eight" means eight plus eight, Gendun Chopel is likely referring to the "sixteen joys" (*dga' ba bcu drug*), an important concept in Buddhist tantra, especially in the *Kālacakra Tantra*. "Immutable vajra bliss" refers to the Kālacakra system of four joys induced through the melting of the drops—joy, supreme joy, joy of absence, and innate joy—into sixteen by correlating the four with body, speech, mind, and wisdom. For a description of this as expounded by Nāropa, see Khedrup Norsang Gyatso, *Ornament of Stainless Light: An Exposition of the Kalacakra Tantra*, trans. Gavin Kilty (Boston: Wisdom Publi-

2. I bow at the feet of Maheśvara,
His beautiful body the color of the stainless sky.
Ever immersed in the glorious play of undying pleasure,
He resides in the snowy ranges of Mount Kailash.

3. I bow at the feet of the goddess Gaurī.
Her beautiful face glows like the full moon,
Her smiling teeth white like a string of pearls,
The nipples of her ample breasts shaped like a conch.

4. This Realm of Desire is the place of passion;
All its creatures seek passion.
The most perfect of all pleasures of passion
Is the bliss of sexual passion of a man and a woman.

5. What man does not desire a woman?
What woman does not desire a man?
Everyone takes delight in this.
They differ only in how they disguise it.

6. In the *Aṅguttara Sūtra* of Laṅkā
These words were spoken by the Lord:
"Among physical forms, the most beautiful
To the eye of a man is the form of a woman. [2][3]

---

cations, 2004), 263. In brief, in this opening stanza, Gendun Chopel is paying homage to the "self-arisen" innate *mahāmudrā*, in which all dualities of subject and object, outer and inner, and saṃsāra and nirvāṇa collapse.

3. Numbers in brackets are the page numbers for the Tibetan text in Gendun Chopel's five-volume collected works, *'Dod pa'i bstan bcos*, in *'Dzam gling rig pa'i dpa' bo mkhas dbang dge 'dun chos 'phel gyi gsung 'bum*, vol. 5 (Hong Kong: Zhang kang gyi ling dpe skrun khang, 2006), 1–72.

7. And to the eye of a woman it is the form of a man.
I have never seen something more beautiful than this.
Among sounds, the most melodious
To the ear of a man is the sound of a woman.

8. To the ear of a woman it is the sound of a man.
There is nothing more pleasing than this."[4]
He said the same about the other three senses:
Fragrances, tastes, and objects of touch.

9. Before the Buddha came into the world,
Many thousands of years ago in the land of India
There were works called "sūtras" and "śāstras"
Among the scriptures of the brahmins.

10. The "Householder's Sūtra," the "Renunciant's Sūtra,"
The "Sūtra on Passion," and so on were there.[5]
They explain the norms of conduct
For renunciants and householders.

11. Spoken by the great sages of the past,
All the traditions of India come from these.

4. This passage is drawn, selectively, from the *Pariyādāna Sutta* of the Aṅguttara Nikāya. However, the original text has an entirely different tone; the term *pariyādāna* means "obsession" in Pāli. Thus, the Buddha says, "No other form do I know, O monks, that so persists in obsessing the mind of a man as the form of a woman." See Nyanaponika Thera and Bhikkhu Bodhi, trans. and eds., *Numerical Discourses of the Buddha: An Anthology of Suttas from the Aṅguttara Nikāya* (Walnut Creek, CA: AltaMira Press, 1999), 33.

5. The first and third texts are clearly the *Gṛhyasūtra* and the *Kāmasūtra*. The second text is *rab tu byung ba'i mdo* in Tibetan, which would be *Pravrājakasūtra* in Sanskrit. Since there is no Hindu text by that name, he is perhaps referring to the *Brahmasūtra*, which advocates the path of renunciation as set forth in the Upaniṣads.

Some sūtras speak of the eighteen sciences.[6]
One of those is this art of lovemaking.

12. In the *Lalitavistara*, when listing the qualities
Suitable to be the bodhisattva's wife,
It says, "Expert in the treatises, like a courtesan."
Knowing the art of lovemaking is counted as well.

13. Elsewhere, when it states "a woman who knows the
treatises,"
It is this treatise [on lovemaking] that it speaks of.
A short *Treatise on Passion* by master Surūpa
Was translated into Tibetan.

14. There is the treatise called *Pleasures of Play*
By the learned brahmin Koka,
Son of Paribhadra, king of Kashmir.[7]
Although it was not translated into Tibetan,
There are some Sanskrit fragments at Ngor Monastery.
There is also one said to be by Nāgārjuna.

(Regarding the sūtras on passion and treatises on pleasure that are well-known today, taking the long and short ones together, there are just over thirty: [3] *Crown Jewel of Kāmadeva* (*Kandarpacūḍāmaṇi*), *Body of the Bodiless One* [i.e., Kāmadeva] (*Anaṅgaraṅga*), *Art of Passion* (*Kāmakalā*), *Secrets of Pleasure* (*Ratirahasya*), *Jeweled Lamp of Pleasure* (*Ratiratnapradīpikā*), and *The Five Arrows* (*Pañcasāyaka*), and so on.)

6. The *Mahāvyutpatti* lists eighteen sciences (*aṣṭadaśavidyāsthānāni, rig pa'i gnas bcu brgyad*), the second of which is *'khrig thabs* (*vaiśika*), literally "methods of intercourse" in Tibetan.

7. This is the *Ratirahasya* by Kokkoka (also known as Koka).

15. Among all of these, the best are two:
Maheśvara's *Treatise on Lust* and
Vātsyāyana's *Sūtra on Passion.*
Here, I base my explanation on these.

16. There are many different types of men,
Yet none not included in these four:
The rabbit type, the stag type,
The bull type, and the horse type.

17. The rabbit type is of moderate size.
Kind-hearted, he has a smiling face.
He does good deeds and has respectable friends.
He renounces sex with the wives of others.

18. He is respectful to the high and helpful to the low.
Enjoying food and clothing that are easily found,
He does not dwell on the past or the future
And is always in a state of idle happiness.

19. His erect member is some six fingerbreadths long.
The jewel's head is soft and round.
His copulation is fast and his semen comes out quickly.
His sweat and semen have a pleasing smell.
There are many of the rabbit type
In good farmlands and pleasant regions.

20. The stag type has bulging eyes and broad shoulders.
He is respectful to his teachers and has good hygiene.
His mind is sharp, and when he walks, he sets off with a jump.
He is always singing and wears fine clothes.

21. He tells the truth and has a large appetite.
He is always hosting feasts for his friends.
He has little hair in his crotch and armpits. [4]
His male organ is some eight fingerbreadths long.
In general, many men of this stag type are found
In all the lands of the earth.

22. The bull type is large with a handsome face.
He is unstable by nature and has little shame.
He makes friends easily; he loses friends easily.
He eats much and knows how to sing and dance.

23. He is wanton in his behavior and very lustful.
He has sex with all the women he can find.
His male organ is some ten fingerbreadths long.
His sweat and semen smell bad.
In general, many of this type live near the sea
And in countries with great plains.

24. The horse type is fat, his body coarse and large.
He has a dark complexion; with long legs, he moves quickly.
He is prone to anger and likes to cheat and lie.
He has relations with all women, whether old or young.

25. This type is extremely lustful.
If they consented, he would even have sex with his mother
and sister.
He will pursue all who are inappropriate,
Like close relatives and the daughters of his gurus.
No matter how much sex he has, his strength never ebbs.
It is hard for him to go even a day without a woman.

26. His member is hard and very thick.
When erect it is some twelve fingerbreadths long.
He has much semen and it smells bad.
There are many of this type in all lands.
However, they are especially prevalent in hot lands
Where rain is rare and the terrain is rugged.

27. If these four basic types just described
Are divided further, there are sixteen.

28. For example, there is the rabbit of the rabbit type,
As well as the stag type of the rabbit type
And the bull and horse types of the rabbit type.
In the same way, the stag type has four. [5]

29. And the bull and horse types each have four.
The subtle differences among these types of men
Can be discerned if scholars analyze them in detail.

30. There are many different types of women,
Yet none not included in these four kinds:
The lotus type and the painting type,
The conch type and the elephant type.

31. The lotus-like is the best type of woman.
Beautiful and with a bright smile, her body is slim and supple.
Free of moles, her complexion is as fair as a swan.
She has long and shining black hair.

32. Her darting eyes are alert like a frightened deer.
Her nostrils are small and her eyebrows thick.
Her clothes are clean, and she likes modest food.
She wears few adornments, like flowers.

33. Her kindness is great and her deeds are virtuous.
She shuns lust for anyone but her spouse.
Her full breasts are soft and round.
Her vagina is some six fingerbreadths deep.
Her menses have the fragrance of a lotus.
This is why she is called the lotus type.

34. Women like Sītā, queen of king Rāma,
Draupadī, wife of the five sons of Pāṇḍu;
Such women are of the lotus type.

35. In general, there were many in ancient times.
They are born into good families
In central regions and fertile lands.

36. The painting type is of average height,
Neither too fat nor too thin,
Her darting long eyes are wide, like lotus petals.
She has a nose like a sesame flower.

37. She wears clothes with striking colors
And puts on garlands of yellow flowers.
She delights in all types of paintings
And likes to listen to amazing tales.

38. She keeps small birds, like parrots
And is always surrounded by children. [6]
Her body is as beautiful as a painting
And so she is called the painting type.

39. She has little interest in the pleasures of sex.
In other ways, she is like the lotus type.
Her vagina is round and eight fingerbreadths deep.
She has little pubic hair and her menses are clear.

40. Pulomā and Rasajñā[8]
Were women of this painting type.
It is said that they are born on the banks of great rivers,
Like the Ganges, Kaveri, and the Indus.

41. The conch type is slim and tall.
She has a curved neck and an upturned nose.
She has a long face and beautiful complexion.
She always eats all sorts of foods.

42. She is skilled in managing her home and servants.
She is eloquent, has a clear mind, and has few secrets.
She easily becomes acquainted with everyone she meets.
It is said that she has little respect for elders
But gets along with those in her own household.

43. Her jealousy and lust are strong.
Her vagina is warm and some ten fingerbreadths deep.
Her pubic hair is thick and her fluids flow easily.
Her body and *bhaga* [vagina] have a sour smell.

44. Most of the women in the world
Belong to this conch type.
Yet due to different qualities and climates of their lands,
They come in many different shapes and colors.
Being talkative, a nimble tongue, and a curved neck,
These are taken to be three sure signs of this type.

45. The elephant type is short, with thick limbs.
Her mouth and nose thick, her hips are wider than others.

8. The Tibetan text here reads "U lo ma ka," presumably meaning Pulomā, the beautiful wife of the sage Bhṛgu. Rasajñā (Ro ldan ma) is possibly the *ḍākinī* consort of Garab Dorje.

Her eyes are red, her hair coarse, her shoulders slump.
Her breasts are large and hard as rocks.
She eats a lot with harsh and annoying sounds.
She covers her body with jewelry in a sloppy way.

46. She likes illicit sex and vulgar talk. [7]
Most of them divorce their spouses.
She enjoys sex with large and strong men
Or anyone she can find.

47. Because she burns with powerful lust,
She wants to have sex with anyone, even her son and father.
She must have sex many times each day.
Some say she cannot be satisfied by a hundred men.

48. Her vagina is hairy and burns like fire.
It is always wet and dripping and smells like a she-elephant.
An adulteress like her is not suitable as a wife.
A hard worker, she is said to be the best of servants.

49. Within these four main types of women,
Again, dividing the four into four, there are sixteen:
The lotus of the lotus type, and so on.
It can be understood as explained above.

50. These sixteen classifications were set forth by Maheśvara.
Vātsyāyana has two groups of three, hence six:
Rabbit, bull, and horse for men;
Deer, mare, and elephant for women.

51. Each of the two groups has the high, middle, and low.
One can understand his system of enumeration in that way.
There are said to be many other modes of classification.
Except for minor differences, they are all similar.

52. Any woman with a red mole
At the base of her left jaw
Will undergo hardship in her youth.
When she reaches thirty she will gain the glory of happiness.

53. If she has a black mole,
She will become happy after she turns forty.
One who has a black mole
At the hairline in the middle of her brow
Is evil by nature and disagrees with her partner.

54. If she has a red mole, she will be loved by her spouse.
If the mole is on the left side of her brow,
She will be loved by all and will find wealth and respect. [8]
If it is on the right side of her brow,
She will not complete any task she undertakes.

55. One who has a string of green moles
Under her left eyebrow,
Will encounter vast wealth.
Pure in her morals, she will be loved by her husband.

56. One who has a red mole at the corner of her eye,
Never separate from sorrow, she will die by the sword.
One who has moles on her cheeks
Will not be very rich but will not be very poor.

57. One who has a mole on her nose
Will journey to faraway lands, succeeding at every undertaking.
It is said that one with a mole on the back of her right jaw
Will constantly undergo great suffering.

58. One who has a mole near her mouth,
Loved by all, she will find resources of food and wealth.

One with a mole in the middle of her throat
Without doubt will become a mistress of wealth.

59. Likewise one with a mole inside her ear
Will be respected by all men even when quarrelsome.
One with a mole on her neck
Will find wealth even in hopeless places.

60. If she has a mole on her left breast,
She will give birth to many girls and suffer.
A woman with a mole on her right breast
Will bear many boys, it is said.

61. One with moles on her right and left shoulders
Will gain power hard for any to suppress.
If she has a mole on her chest, she will be ill willed.
If she has a mole on her belly, her appetite will be great.

62. Whatever marks of virtue or sin
On the left side of a woman's body
Mean the opposite
On the right side of a man.
However, none of this is very trustworthy.

63. Women younger than twelve
Are referred to as girls.
They should be given betel leaves and sweets
And told about the pleasures of kissing. [9]

64. From the age of thirteen to twenty-five,
She is said to be in the prime of life.
She should be kissed, scratched, and so on.
Seeking her company, one should enjoy her with pleasure.

65. From the age of twenty-six to fifty,
She is referred to as a mature woman.
Offer her erotic talk, bites, and scratches,
Likewise give her the riches of passion.

66. Women past the age of fifty
Are referred to as old women.
They should be listened to and addressed with respect
And asked for good advice about the present and future.

67. Among humans born on earth in this Realm of Desire,
There are two conflicting classes: men and women; they desire each other.
The pleasure of passion is supreme among all pleasures.
Yet it is easily found by all, the high and the humble.

68. Because men and women are so different,
If they were not brought together by coupling,
The world would be split into two factions
Always in conflict and at war.

69. Monks who live in forest retreats
May not know the value of this.
Yet even the human form with eighteen conditions[9]
First comes about through sex.

9. Gendun Chopel is referring here to the eighteen conditions of "leisure and opportunity" (*dal 'byor*) of an auspicious rebirth as a human. "Leisure" refers to freedom from the eight conditions of nonleisure: birth in hell, birth as a ghost, birth as an animal, birth in an uncivilized place, having defective sense organs, having wrong views, birth as a god of long life, birth in a world where a buddha has not appeared. "Opportunity" refers to being born with five inner fortunes and the five outer fortunes. The first are: being a human, being born in a place where Buddhism flourishes, having nondefective sense organs, not having committed one of the five deeds of immediate retribution (killing one's father, killing one's

70. If sex were abandoned in the realm of humans,
It would surely become empty in an instant.
And if there were no human beings,
How could there be monks and the Buddha's teachings?

71. The six ornaments and the two supreme ones[10] appeared in the land of India.
The teacher Shenrap[11] was born in the region of Olmo.
The Ming emperor was born in a palace in China.
There is no need to explain where they first came from.

72. "The brahmin caste came from the mouth of Brahmā."
This is what the Hindu texts say. [10]
How can this be true, when all four castes were born from the wombs of women?
No one, wise or foolish, can deny this.

73. A man and woman, though bereft of wealth and power,
Find the bliss of heaven in their bed.
Even an old man, with hair whiter than a conch,
Finds inexpressible joy in the womb of his old wife.

74. Not spitefully binding or beating someone,
Not cruelly stabbing someone with a spear;

---

mother, killing an *arhat*, wounding a buddha, and causing dissent in the monastic community), and having faith in the Buddhist scriptures. The five outer fortunes are: a buddha appearing in the world, his teaching the dharma, the dharma remaining to the present day, his followers existing, and the people of the region having love and compassion and teaching others.

10. The six ornaments are Nāgārjuna and Āryadeva, Asaṅga and Vasubandhu, and Dignāga and Dharmakīrti; the two supreme ones are the vinaya masters, Guṇaprabha and Śākyaprabha.

11. Shenrap is the buddha of the Bön tradition.

Passion is offered to a passionate human.
It may not be a virtue, but how could it be a sin?

75. "To give a woman to a desirous man
Is supreme among all gifts."
This is stated in the *sādhana* chapter of the *Kālacakra Tantra*.[12]
If you do not believe it, look; it is clearly there.

76. A beggar may turn up his nose at gold.
A hungry guest may spit at his meal.
Though everyone condemns sex with their mouth,
Just this is the place of pleasure in their mind.

77. Only the rich acquire gold, silver, horses, and cattle.
The enjoyment of sex is found by all, high and humble.
Sunlight, wind, earth, and water,
Whatever is precious is shared by all.

78. Whatever miracles that occur on earth are done by humans.
Humans are produced by sex between a man and a woman.
When considered this way, what deed has greater meaning
Than the union of the two organs?

79. For a deed of such great importance,
There is no need to be exhorted to struggle.
All men and women do this naturally.
This is the law set forth by the king, dependent origination.

12. Gendun Chopel may be referring here to the passage in the *Kālacakra Tantra*, "yid 'ong chung ma skal bzangs bu mo rnams kyang gsang ba sbyin pa la ni rab sbyin bya." See *Mchog gi dang po'i sangs rgyas las phyung ba'i rgyud kyi rgyal po dpal dus kyi 'khor lo*, chap. 4, stanza 205d; Kangyur D, rgyud ka, 98b5.

80. Does it not amaze you that,
Without studying the arts and sciences,
A living statue of the dharma master Butön[13] was made
By a half hour of lovemaking in bed?

81. The magic of causes and conditions coming together is amazing indeed.
The magic of man and woman coming together is more amazing than that. [11]
That this marvelous science is naturally known by all fools, without study,
This indeed is the most amazing of all.

82. To deny that the amazing is amazing;
Sakya Lama said this is the sign of a fool.[14]
Of course, these days I am a madman.
But those who are not mad can go ahead and laugh at me.

83. The experience of bliss is no small matter.
The creation of families is no small matter.
If the path of passion can be sustained within bliss and emptiness,
How could that be a small matter?

13. Butön (Bu ston, 1290–1364) was an eminent Tibetan scholar who was an early compiler of the Tibetan Buddhist canon. Gendun Chopel's point here is that an extraordinary Buddhist master who would someday be immortalized in statues was created by something as ordinary as thirty minutes of lovemaking.

14. Sakya Lama here refers to the Tibetan master Sakya Paṇḍita (1182–1251). This statement is found in his *Treasury of Eloquent Advice* (*Legs bshad rin po che'i gter*, better known as *Sa skya legs bshad*), chap. 3, stanza 36. The full stanza reads: "Ignorant of good and bad, they forget others' kindness. They do not grasp amazing speech as amazing. They keep asking others what they can actually see. Cowardly and gullible, these are the signs of a fool." For an English translation of Sakya Paṇḍita's text, see John T. Davenport, trans., *Ordinary Wisdom: Sakya Pandita's Treasury of Good Advice* (Boston: Wisdom Publications, 2000).

84. For every man there is a woman.
For every woman there is a man.
The minds of both desire their union.
What chance is there of remaining celibate?

85. When suitable deeds are prohibited in public,
Unsuitable deeds will be done in private.
How can religious and secular laws
Suppress this natural desire of humans?

86. This bliss abides in its natural state
In the system of channels endowed with five wheels,
In the vajra city of six essences.
How is it right to call it a fault and prevent it?

87. To delight in the desired is attachment.
To delight in the desired is faith.
To fear the undesired is anger.
To fear the undesired is renunciation.

88. To desire and not desire are attributes of the mind.
They can be changed; they cannot be abandoned.
When analyzed with care, this taking the afflictions
As the path is a way of all the vehicles.[15]

89. For one's own welfare or the general welfare of the realm,
For the reign of a king or the livelihood of a beggar,

15. Gendun Chopel is here challenging the traditional assertion that the method of taking the afflictions as the path is unique to the Vajrayāna. His argument is that, if *faith* can be defined as a form of delight in an admirable object, it is a form of desire. If *renunciation* is a fear of saṃsāra, it is a form of aversion. Thus, two negative emotions—desire and aversion—are attributes of the path. Thus even in the Hīnayāna, there is a form of practice that brings the afflictions to the path.

Whatever deed one might perform, great or small,
It cannot be done without a woman.

90. Making prayers for what one desires
And performing rituals to the gods on high; [12]
When these are done with women,
They are said to grant results swiftly without fail.

91. This wide world is like a desert plain.
People grow weary with the burden of so many deeds.
A woman playmate who can bring joy there
Is like a magical creation of one's deeds.

92. She is the *goddess* who brings joy to your mind when you see her.
She is the *field* where good families grow.
She is the *nurse* who cares for you when you are sick.
She is the *poet* who consoles you when your mind is weary.

93. She is the *maid* who does all the work of the house.
She is the *partner* who sustains you with love in this life.
Your wife with whom you are linked by deeds gathered in the past
Is endowed with these six attributes.

94. "Women are unstable and promiscuous."
Such statements are utterly false.
In adultery there is no difference between men and women.
If one considers it carefully, men are even worse.

95. A king takes a thousand queens;
Still this is proclaimed a virtue.
If a woman had a hundred bridegrooms,
She would be insulted as if it were unheard of.

96. If he makes love to the thousand women in turn,
How can this be infidelity?
Since making love to one's wife is not adultery,
How can there be adultery for rich men?

97. A rich old man with hair the color of snow
Selects a young woman and buys her.
She is a commodity sold for a price.
Alas, women have no companion to protect them.

98. When a man takes a woman by force,
She does not come to him by her own wish.
This is like patching wood with a piece of stone.
How can such a woman be loyal?

99. In the land of Persia, each old man
Takes five young brides.
The moment one of the brides commits adultery
She is burned alive and killed. [13]

100. One man can be satisfied by five women
But how can five be satisfied by one old man?
Thus in the many kingdoms of the world
There are many laws to suit the desires of the rich.

101. These are given the name "civilized dharma,"
Because they accord with the wishes of the king.
The scholars just nod and smile.
When you think about it, there is no end to despair.

102. Thus, do not listen only to the shouts
Proclaimed in a single voice by men of the same class.
Bear witness to the reasons for what is true;
At least proclaim what is honest and right.

103. Her father's house where she was born is not her permanent abode.
It is hard to take care of herself, seeking her own way.
A woman is like a doe in a barren land.
Her companion for a lifetime is her husband.

104. In the land of India each morning
The wife bows at her husband's feet.
Mixing dust from his feet with *sindhura*,[16]
She puts a red dot on her forehead.

105. In Nepal, even if a man takes a woman by force
And carries out his lust,
As soon as he is finished, she stands up,
Touches his feet with her head and leaves.

106. At first, she struggles a great deal, saying, "No."
Afterwards, she bows and says, "You are most kind."
Thinking about this, I feel like laughing.
Yet they say this is a respectable practice.

107. Her husband sustains her with whatever food, clothes, and jewelry she wants,
And guides her in everything she does in life.
For women there is no higher religious practice
Than to honor and worship her husband.

108. A woman may abandon her husband
To practice charity or asceticism,
Yet all the virtues done without his permission
Will not produce great karmic effects. [14]

16. A red powder.

109. A woman should adopt all the attitudes
That her husband's mind finds beautiful,
And through various actions of passion and pleasure,
She should deeply merge her body and mind with his.

110. A prostitute shuns her husband's protection;
She is a defiled woman physically and ethically.
It is said that the touch of a breeze that bears dust from her feet
Makes the pure gods frightened and flee.

111. Half of a husband's body is his wife
And half of a wife's body is her husband.
If one's body were cut in half, having only human arms and legs,
It would be hard even to include it among animals.

112. Thinking in this way, if you can maintain
A loving attitude toward your spouse free from hypocrisy,
And reach the end of this short life,
Even the bare bones of your corpse will be worthy of worship.

113. Abandoning the various forms of sexual misconduct
Such as praising as proper what is improper,
To leave the imprint of intercourse on a woman's breast [i.e.,
a child],
This is the dharma of a civilized world.

114. Although much is said about the types of women
Who are suitable and unsuitable for intercourse,
For the most part, it is best to follow
The customs of each region.

115. The Indians make a great prohibition:
"One does not have sex with a widow."

When analyzed rationally, I see no reason not to;
In fact, I see great benefit.
Thus, one should have intercourse
With young widows whose mourning has ended.

116. The custom of not meeting with a man
Until three full years have passed after the spouse has died
Can be seen in many lands.
This is a civilized custom and should be followed if possible.

117. There are also some rules that say
That because a widow is unclean [15]
One should not eat food prepared by her.
This is a saying of heartless brahmins.

> (In the pledges associated with [the propitiation rites of] Devī and Vaiśravaṇa, it speaks of such things as not eating food from the hand of a widow.)[17]

118. In ancient times in the land of India, when their husbands died
Women would jump into the flames and die.
If she could not kill herself, though living, she would be considered a corpse.
This is the source of the idea that a widow is polluting.

119. Inside the body, everyone is polluted.
On the outside, everyone is covered with skin.
These many distinctions of pure and impure among people
Can be traced back to the Hindu religion.

17. Gendun Chopel is speaking here of the propitiation rites of protective deities such as Palden Lhamo (referred to here as Devī) and the god of wealth, Vaiśravaṇa.

120. Also, there are many statements about forbidden partners,
Such as close relatives of the same bloodline.
Yet these are just the customs of various kingdoms.
It is hard to be certain about who is suitable and who is not.

121. However, having sex with the wife of another
Destroys harmony and is the source of strife.
Causing suffering in this life and the next, it is a shameless deed.
Respectable people should avoid it like a contagious disease.

122. Though the *Kāmasūtra* says that it is suitable
To have sex with a wife whose husband is far away,
It leads to the birth of illegitimate children
And similar faults described earlier; it should be shunned.

123. The followers of master Bābhravya say
That there is no fault in having sex with any woman
Except the wife of a brahmin or one's guru.
This is a shameless lie and deception.
Most of the authors of the ancient treatises were brahmins.
They always wrote things like this.

> (Similarly, in order to purify the sins of a woman, they explain the rite called *kāmavrata*. It is said that after allowing herself to be enjoyed by a brahmin for thirteen months, she still has to give him gifts like parasols, gold, and cows.) [16]

124. Presentations in deceitful treatises such as these
Will be discerned if the intelligent dispute the scriptures.
It is clearly stated in the *Kālacakra Tantra*
That brahmins are vicious about their wives.

125. There are a great many lands.
In some, uncle and niece are together,
In others, brother and sister, or first cousins.
The custom of the land itself is what is considered pure.

(In some border regions of northwest India, when the father dies, the mother stays with the son. To be truthful, the reference to a "treatise on taking one's mother as a bride" is clearly referring to the Highest Yoga Tantras. These tantras flourished first in regions such as Oḍḍiyāna; the people of that region belong to the Patan clan. Although Dharmakīrti and Bhāviveka were later included into the list of *mahāsiddhas,* when one looks at the works of each of these masters, it is clear that, in addition to not being familiar with Mantra, they completely reject it. For example, in the autocommentary to the *Pramāṇavārttika,* [Dharmakīrti] gives an example of why it is not necessary to be a good person in order to compose a text, saying that these days *ḍākinīs* and demons are seen composing tantras. Similarly, in the *Tarkajvālā,* [Bhāviveka] expresses his contempt for the performance of the initiation rite of Īśvara from the tip of a *liṅga* [penis]. He writes, "Something that even when its name is heard / People are utterly embarrassed."[18] If he were familiar with [Buddhist] Mantra, how could he not be ashamed of things that are similar, like our own secret initiation and knowledge initiation? Thus, since Vajrayāna had just spread at that time to Oḍḍiyāna and Lambaka, which were controlled by the Patan clan, I do not think that we need have any doubt that the "treatise on taking one's mother as a bride" is anything other than a [Buddhist] tantra.) [17]

18. *Tarkajvālā* (*Rtog ge 'bar ba*), chap. 8; Tengyur D, dbu ma dza, 293a1. The full citation reads: "gang gi ming thos skye bo'i tshogs / shin tu ngo tshar 'gyur ba yi / gang las mi gtsang tshogs 'byung ba / de ni lha yin ji ltar 'dod / shin tu ngo tshar med gyur pas / mtshan ma'i rtse nas dbang skur bas / gang gis bdag nyid co 'dri ba / de las lhag pa ci zhig bya."

126. Having sex forcefully with a young girl
Causes great pain at the site
And the inside of the *bhaga* can be wounded,
Bringing difficulties later during childbirth.

127. If it is not the right time and there is danger due to lust,
Rub [the penis] between her thighs and release yourself.
This is a custom in many places
And causes a young girl to mature quickly.

128. Cover the outside of a rolled up cloth
With salve and make a small soft tip.
Every day raise her passion
And then put it just inside the *bhaga*.

129. Finally, put in the *liṅga*.
If the girl is not fully mature,
Rub butter on the *liṅga*
And put it in slowly.

130. If one rubs the *liṅga* between the thighs,
The *bhaga* will naturally blossom and mature, so they say.
There are other instructions on how to tame a girl.
Since they are not needed in our country I shall leave
these out.

131. The *Caitra* month is the first of the months.
If the lotus is opened in this month,
It is said that she will be respected by all,
But will quickly separate from her husband.

132. The girl whose lotus is opened in the *Vaiśākha* month
Will have mostly virtuous thoughts.

Her behavior pure, she will be loved by her lord.
She will be wondrous in religious practice and wealth.

133. The girl whose lotus is opened in the *Jyaiṣṭha* month
Will encounter great amounts of wealth.
She will find a husband who is handsome and brave
And he will be loving toward her.

134. The girl whose lotus is opened in the *Āṣāḍha* month
Will be afflicted with illness and have no children,
But she will sustain her loving nature
And will always practice charity.

135. The girl whose lotus is opened on the *Vaiśākha* full moon
Will have insatiable lust.
Every child she bears will die in infancy. [18]
But if she is protected by a *nāga* this will be reversed, it's said.

136. The girl whose lotus is opened in the *Bhādrapada* month
Will undergo unbearable sorrow.
Her body will be afflicted with various diseases
And she will die in poverty and destitution, it's said.

137. The girl whose lotus is opened in the *Āśvina* month
Will be respectful toward her husband.
She will bear many children and some will die young,
But she will never be destitute through lacking wealth.

138. The girl whose lotus is opened in the *Kārttika* month,
Her mother's family will be poor.
However, if she lives with her husband,
She will attain glory and happiness, it's said.

139. The girl whose lotus is opened in the *Mārgaśīrṣa* month
Will be loving toward her husband.
She will make offerings to renunciants pure in ethics,
And will thrive in the path of the pure religion.

140. The girl whose lotus is opened in the *Pauṣa* month
Will be skilled in the work of the household.
Clear in mind, she will know the *śāstras*.
She will be loved by her husband and respected by all.

141. The girl whose lotus is opened in the *Māgha* month
Will be gloriously wealthy.
She will engage in all her deeds with a sense of wonder
And she will sustain renunciants and her poor relatives.

142. The girl whose lotus is opened in the *Phālguna* month
Will be happy, rich, and will practice the dharma.
She will be loved by her husband and will have many sons
And they will be victorious on the earth.

143. Because Arjuna was born in this month,
It is known as the best among the twelve months.
Sometimes these are applied to young girls
As the effect of their first menstruation.

> (It seems that in both southern India and Sinhala, there is the custom that at the time of a young girl's first menstruation, brahmins are summoned, offerings are made, and a great feast is arranged in the home for the relatives.)

144. A male comes of age at sixteen
And is complete at twenty-four. [19]

A female comes of age at thirteen
And is complete at sixteen.

145. Thus, when a man is twenty-four
And a woman is sixteen or eighteen,
The appropriate time for sex arrives.
From this point also they start a family.

146. If one delays sex too long from this age,
Some kinds of diseases will occur, it's said.
If a boy has sex with a woman when he is too young,
He will lose his strength and age quickly.

147. However, if a woman meets a man at a young age,
It is said that this slows her aging.
This isn't just something I made up;
They say it is confirmed by experiences of old men and women.

148. The relentless suffering of lust
Aches in the bones all day and night.
For a human in the prime of life, this suffering is great.
But the old always make light of it.

149. For girls guarded by parents and living by their rules,
There is no suffering greater than this.
Thus, when the appropriate time comes
Men and women must marry.

150. The need of a thirsty man to find water
Does not compare to the lust of a young girl for a man.
The hunger for food of a starving man
Does not compare to the lustful man's thoughts about a woman.

151. Being thrown into a deep dungeon
Is not as bad as being hindered by stern parents.
Being placed in stocks in prison
Is not as bad as making strict religious laws about it.

152. If the thought of renunciation has been perfected,
Water held back by a dam continues to flow.
Yet if one levies the tax of an unwanted religious law,
[Abstinence] is like pushing a boulder uphill.

153. A husband and wife, each produced by the other's karma,
Should love each other like they cherish life itself, [20]
Abandoning acts of deception and adultery;
This is the pinnacle of all ethics.

154. When one's vital essence is spent and the mind is at peace,
A gray-haired man together with his wife
Strive at the path of religion in a forest retreat.
This was the practice of noble old men in ancient times.

155. Thus, as long as the horse of the senses runs wild
And has the power to enter the land of passion,
One should rely on the enjoyment of lust.
How could a thinking person condemn this?

156. Seeking livelihood from labor that accords with the
dharma,
Always making love to only one's wife,
Taming the senses and enjoying a feast from time to time,
In the home of such an excellent man, liberation is found.

| (This final stanza comes from the *Cāṇakyaśāstra*.)

157. The essence of the human body is blood;
The concentrated essence of blood is semen.
Physical strength, mental clarity, and so on
Depend for the most part on this vital essence.

158. If, through various physical diseases
Or through relations with a prostitute,
The causal semen is damaged,
The lineage of sons will end.

159. No children will be born to a mother by such a father,
And even if children are born, they will quickly die.
If they do not die, they will have physical defects.
Therefore, one should take care with such behavior.

160. If physical things are stirred and rubbed,
It is their nature to release their essence.
When clouds are churned, a stream of rain falls.
When sticks are rubbed together, a tongue of flame appears.

161. Likewise, although the essence of milk is butter,
At first, it remains mixed with milk.
But when milk is poured in a pail and churned,
The milk gradually becomes warm
And its inner essence comes out and separates. [21]

162. In the same way, semen is blood's essence,
But at first it remains absorbed in the blood.
When a man and woman unite and begin churning,
The blood is heated by the power of passion,
And semen, like butter, emerges.

163. Seven drops of the essence of food
Produce one drop of blood in the human body.
From a cup full of blood
Just one subtle drop of semen is produced.

164. Because women lose blood each month
Their strength is small and their flesh soft and loose.
Their skin is thin and very sensitive.
When they age, their body has many wrinkles.

165. Yet apart from mere external aspects
There is no difference at all in the bodies of men and women.
There is nothing in a male body
That women do not also possess.

166. Even the two balls are found inside the womb.
The labia on the sides of the *bhaga*
Are the layer of skin gathered at the base of a *liṅga*.
Beneath it is a small piece of flesh the size of a finger.

167. When passion is aroused, it becomes erect and hard.
This is the equivalent of the male member.
And when it is touched with the finger and rubbed
Lust quickly rises in women.

168. When making love, it's said that in that very flesh,
The painful itch of passion is especially intense.
The two layers [of skin] that divide in half at the scrotum
Are found at the sides of the *bhaga*.

169. Likewise, a man has a womb in his belly.
There is also the cause for breasts swelling on his chest.

(When he is young, a male starts to swell slightly and then
shrinks again.)
The crack visible on the head of the penis
Is just a closed remnant of the female mark.

170. "Women of Sindhu, Persia, and Oḍḍiyāna have great desire."
This is very well known
On the face of this earth. [22]
Their anther [clitoris] is very thick.

171. At times it would protrude outside the *bhaga*
Making it possible to have sex with other women.
Often, it is about the size of the male member.
It can sometimes be seen outside the [female] mark.

172. In general, a woman from the Western lands
Is beautiful, brilliant, and braver than others.
Her behavior is said to be coarse, her face like a man's.
She even has little whiskers around her mouth.

173. These fierce and fearless women
Can only be tamed by lust.
Because they can suck the *liṅga* during sex
Western woman are known as semen drinkers.

174. She resorts to dogs, bulls, and different animals,
Even to her own father and son.
She has no qualms about following anyone
Who is able to give her the enjoyments of sex.

175. Some women who have a thick anther
Have both marks or are changing hermaphrodites.
There are many women who can turn into men

With the slightest physical change.
There are also men whose *liṅga* disappears deep inside
So that they turn into women.

176. If one has a wife with powerful passion
It is certain one will have a family of all sons.
Those who seek sons and the enjoyment of pleasure
Should choose and take a passionate woman.

177. For example, the soft and shriveled Rumex plant
Becomes stiff and swollen when soaked by rain.
In the same way, when drops of blood gather together
The male and female organs become erect and swollen.

178. When pleasure is produced in the secret region
The focus of the mind goes there.
As a result, the vital winds and blood gather there.
Filling the inside of the organ, the *liṅga* becomes erect.

179. A man's passion is light and easily raised. [23]
A woman's passion is deep and hard to arouse.
Thus various practices of passion should be used
To rouse a woman's passion.

180. It's said that the anther of the *bhaga* and its inner part,
As well as the skin on the left and right of the opening,
The mouth of the womb and the tips of the breasts,
These become erect and swell when passion is produced.

181. For men, it is the entire *liṅga*,
As well as the shaft up to the edge of pubic hair
Where sensations of pleasure arise when passion is produced.
The most essential part is at the head of the *liṅga*.

182–83. Yet the pleasure of women
Is widely dispersed and cannot be defined.
From below the belly down to the thighs,
The interior of the *bhaga* and the entrance of the womb,
The anus and the cheeks of the buttocks,
In short, all of the lower half of the body, inside and out,
Can feel and be filled with the pleasure of sex.
A woman's entire body is said to be her female mark.

184. As to whether or not a woman has semen,
The explanations all disagree.
The *Sūtra to Nanda on Entering the Womb*
And the new translation tantras say that they do.

185. The followers of master Bābhravya say
That when women engage in sex
They emit semen from start to finish.

186. Thus if the pleasures of passion were to be apportioned,
The female has a hundred times more, they say.
Yet others say that they are confusing
The moistness of passion for semen.

187. Wherever the power of the mind is drawn to,
The channels of that organ come together
And the inner fluids are squeezed out.
When one thinks of delicious food, one salivates.

188. When one burns with shame, sweat comes from the body.
When passion is produced, fluid boils from the genitals.
When one is happy or sad, tears come from the eyes. [24]

189. Thus, when passion, sorrow, and the like
Are stopped as they begin to arise in the mind,
There is no fault; it is very good to do so.

190. But when they have become strong and powerful,
If one forcefully stops them, this leads to repressed anger.[19]
This is the reason why all who seem dignified from the outside
Have so much repressed anger.

191. Even if women do have semen,
It flows gradually like melting ice.
It does not come spurting out quickly at once
In the way that is does for us men.

192. Thus, it is not the case that the moment it comes out
Women are satisfied and have a feeling of revulsion.
It does not feel itchy and unbearable
If one continues to thrust after emission.

193. A woman once told me, as the fluids gradually flow,
Because the inside of the *bhaga* becomes moist and sensitive,
The pleasure is especially great.
I think that what Bābhravya said is true.

194. The master Kumāriputra said no difference exists
Between men and women in how semen emerges.
Most knowledgeable people today
And women learned in many texts,
Say that the female has no semen.

19. The Tibetan term Gendun Chopel uses is *snying rlung*, which literally means "heart wind." In Tibetan folk psychology *snying rlung* refers to a kind of a repressed anger that makes the person restless and irritable.

195. Because I like to talk about what lies below the waist,
I have asked many of my female friends about this.
Other than scornful laughs and being hit with fists,
I could not find even one who would give an honest answer.

196. Although Yangchen Dolma would speak honestly,
She herself does not seem to be that sure.
From my perspective, even if women have no semen
They do have something they release.

197. Whether it is a kind of fluid or a type of air,
If an experienced old man investigates, he will know.
For women, too, on each occasion of intercourse
The pleasure of climax arises each time. [25]

198. When engaging in sex several times,
The first time, the man's semen is emitted quickly
And the power of sexual passion is great.

199. For women, it is the opposite.
The first time, their passion is weak.
It is said to grow greater each time.

200. Thus, a man who does not emit his semen for a long time,
Whose member is strong and does not weaken quickly
Is said to give the glory of passion [to women].
This is what women discuss at home.

201. When you have an itch on a part of your body,
If you scratch it with your finger, you feel content.
It is said that this is how female pleasure is fulfilled.

202. However, it is said that at the time of intercourse,
The pleasure of a woman is seven times greater [than a man].
When his semen comes out, the pleasure of a man is complete.
When her itching ends, the pleasure of a woman is complete.

203. Therefore, if he engages in passion many times,
The body of a man becomes quite taxed.
But the body of a woman is not harmed at all.

204. The inside of the *bhaga* and the small fleshy anther
Are naked flesh without any cover.
Thus, like touching an open wound,
The pleasure and pain of women is intense.

205. And so, there are many different ways
That the pleasure of passion is produced in men and women.
Other than how it is experienced in one's own mind,
One cannot describe it to another saying, "It is like this."

206. The women of Ujjayanī
Delight in amazing pictures.
[In foreplay] they only embrace and kiss,
But they are skilled in the palanquin position.

207. The women of Sindhu suck the male member
And experience extraordinary pleasure.
The women of Lāṭa gasp and moan.
They have burning passion and a rough nature. [26]
It is said that the loud "ooh" sound they make at the time of passion
Can be heard beyond the boundary of three fences.

208. The Gandhāra women have a fair complexion and moderate body size.
Their hips are large and their *bhaga* completely covered.
They drink a bright and delicious beer
And always pass their time talking about sex.

209. From the *bhaga* of the Draviḍa women
A white fluid emerges before making love.
In the lands of Gauḍa and Kāmarūpa,
The women are very loose.
It is said that if a man just touches their hand
They will follow him and give him pleasure.

210. The women of Gujarat
Have darting eyes and thin and sad-looking bodies.
Their breasts are large and their hair is like flowers.
They are filled with lust outside and inside.

211. Because the female mark of the women
Of the city of Yāma itches intensely from time to time,
They ask men to have sex with them
Or use a male member made of wood.
It is said that in lands controlled only by women
They always indulge in sex acts in this way.

212. The girls in Koṅkana in the south
Do not see their own faults but criticize others.
They themselves bite and scratch,
But if a man does so they mock him.

213. The women of Aṅga, Vaṅga, and Kaliṅga
Are the queens of sexual passion.
They like to bite and scratch

And like to be treated roughly.
They are never satisfied however many times they have sex
And always keep concealed a male member made of leather.

214. Except for the city of Pāṭaliputra,
The girls of the cities of Magadha,
On the shores of the Gaṅgā and Yamunā,
Give birth to noble lineages and have a peaceful manner.
And at the time of sex, they do not even like to kiss;
Biting and scratching would be inappropriate. [27]

215. The women of Rāṣṭra in the west
Have a passionate nature that burns like fire.
During sex they cry and bite.
They indulge in all sixty-four [arts of love].

216. They like varieties of lovemaking,
And satisfy themselves through amazing acts.
They suck the man's organ
And make bite marks on his body.

217. The women of Pāṭaliputra
Also have a nature of burning passion,
But are discreet and unpretentious.
They only have sex in secret.

218. The women of Bāhanika, Malaya in the south,
And the land of five rivers [Punjab]
Enjoy embracing and kissing.
It is said they need a long time for sex.

219. The girls of Bāhlika are ravishing.
Caressing one, she has intercourse with another.

Kissing another, she rubs the organ of another.
It is said that she can play with five men at once.
In the same way, all the parts of a man's body
Can be satisfied at the same time by many women.

220. In Vidarbha women have no family guardians.
They have sex with everyone, whether suitable or not.
The women of Sāketa and Saurasena are all
Accustomed to oral sex (*mukhamaithuna*).

221. Also, most women on the banks of the Candrabhāgā River
Are perceived as liking it.
When the women of Arhara have sex
They constantly squeeze their *bhaga*, like a trotting mare.

222. In the land of Cola, they enjoy fierce sex,
Hitting and biting like a mad person.
It is said that a girl named Citrasenā died
With her entire body wounded in this way.

223. The girls in the kingdom of Aparānta in western India
Are unreliable and are lovers for only a short time. [28]
The girls of the land of Kembajali
Are highly skilled in the opening and closing of their *bhaga*.

224. It is said that they are able to give the full pleasure of sex
Even if the man's organ is small and not erect.
In general, it appears that men in that region
Have small members and weak bodies.

225. The Laṅkā women have a bluish complexion and flexible waists.
Though their *bhaga* is loose, they are skilled in the tricks of movement.

They enjoy sex, embracing the man
By wrapping their legs around his neck.

226. The field-born farm girls of Kunlanta
Are strong and fat with hard breasts and *bhaga*.
The girls of Suvarṇadvīpa have beautiful faces.
They make love like a corpse, without moving.
Likewise the women of the southeast regions
Are said to be deficient in the enjoyments of sex.

227. The women of Kapila and Oḍḍiyāna
Have the nature of flesh-eating demons.
With *bhagas* like fire, their fluids are always boiling.
Their passion unbearable, they act as if they were mad.

228. In Kuru and the land of Kanyakubja,
The western region where seven rivers flow,
And the valleys of Kusha in the Muslim kingdom,
It is said there are so many beautiful girls.

229. Among the women who drink the waters of the Himalayan snows
Billowing down from rocky mountain peaks,
Carrying the essence of the king of the lizards,
There are those who possess the essence of fire within.

230. Most of these are stated in the *Kāmasūtra*.
All of these places are in India alone.
Furthermore, these are traditions from ancient times;
There is no certainty that things are like this today.

231. The master Suvarṇanābha says that
Because the races congregate in various cities,
Women learn each other's practices

And so everything is always changing.
Still, it is certainly true that in each of the regions [29]
The nature of people has remained mostly the same.

232. Thus, this nature of women
Should be explained, applying it to Tibetan women.
But I am familiar only with Kham and Tsang women;
I cannot write in detail about their qualities.

233. Kham women have soft flesh and are fond of passion.
Tsang women are skilled and are good at lifting up from underneath.
I have written this casual catalog of Tibetan women
In order to inspire other lustful ones.

234. As to how the women of Amdo, Kham, Ü, Tsang, and Ngari
Lie down, how they move, and so on [when making love],
An old monk who knows about the world
Or anyone who knows may add it here.

Two

TYPES OF EMBRACE

235. Like a timid thief eating a meal in hiding,
To churn in and out and then ejaculate
Silently and quietly in a darkened bed,
This is not a true celebration of sexual passion.

236. Thus one should know passion's sixty-four arts,
Which offer various flavors of pleasure,
To the passionate man and woman,
Like the flavors of molasses, milk, and honey.

237. One who is learned in the postures of passion
Can craze the mind of a man.
One who can befuddle him at times of bliss,
She is called the best of women.

238. Embracing, kissing, scratching, biting,
Hitting, moaning, ways of copulating, a man's acts [by a woman],

Each of these eight is divided into eight.
There are sixty-four arts of passion. [30]

239. There is sucking, slapping, caressing with the tongue,
And the wondrous act of oral sex (*mukhamaithuna*).
It is said that for the passionate woman
There are unspecified acts beyond number.

240. Seeking a reason to flirt,
One touches the bare shoulder of a stranger
In tight corridors or when taking or placing things.
This is known as *spṛṣṭaka* or touching.

241. In a secluded place, she leans down with her arms
At the level of her lover's neck
And touches him with the tips of her breasts.
This is known as *viddhaka* or piercing.

242. Wildly driven by unknown passions,
He pushes her against the wall
Biting her cheek and the top of her shoulder.
This is known as *pīḍitaka* or crushing.

243. She wraps her arms around his neck,
And while they touch each other at their bellies,
He holds her and lifts her up.
This is *latāsveṣṭha*, the circling creeper.

244. She rests one leg around his waist.
With the other she presses the top of his foot,
And bending his head with her hand, they kiss.
This is known as *climbing the tree*.

245. Bound together thigh to thigh,
She presses her breasts against his chest
And moves her upper body, staring into his eyes.
This is called the *palm tree swayed by the wind*.

246. At the end of sex, standing or lying down,
With an all-consuming passion like burning fire,
They press their lower bodies together, then unite.
This is called the *fluttering banner*.

247. Both shrouded in the haze of passion,
Chest joined to chest, organ joined to organ,
They make love naked in bed.
This is known as *mixing water and milk*.

248. Women who are aroused by such varieties
Let down their hair, kiss, and stroke the *liṅga*.
Free of pretense or shame,
They truly become wish-granting cows.

Three

ACTS OF KISSING

249. When he meets a woman he has known before,
At first, with smiles of delight,
They touch each other's cheeks and kiss.
This is "getting to know each other" or *pratibodha*.

250. For a girl whose face is sullied with sadness,
Scratch her around the neck,
Kiss her ear and the crown of her head.
These types are called the first kisses.

251. Then, a young girl who is drinking both
The beer of passion and the honey of shame,
Kisses with trembling lips that open and close.
This is known as *sphuritaka* or throbbing.

252. When a woman changes her behavior
And drags her lips and tongue over his body,

This is a sign of pleasure produced.
It is called *nimittaka* or having a sign.

253. Cursed by passion, her eyes change.
Placing her cheek on his nose, she kisses him
And the tip of her tongue caresses the inside of his mouth.
This is known as the waterwheel, *ghaṭika*.

254. He kisses all nine places on her body.
As soon as he has done so,
She answers with kisses on those places of the man.
This is called *uttara* or after-kiss.

255. He sucks and kisses
Her belly [while she lies] on her back.
The corner of his cheek rubs the hollow of her waist.
This is the *piṭaka* or a small box. [32]

256. A woman drunk with passion and unsated
Kisses the swollen *liṅga* of the man.
When his pleasure is forced out, she drinks it drunkenly.
Thus, roughly, there are eight varieties of kissing.

257. The ear, the throat, the cheek, the armpit, the lips,
The thighs, the belly, the breasts, the *bhaga*—
These nine sensitive places are said to be the places to kiss.
Your own mind will show you what is right.

258. Especially, the area between the breasts and knees
Are tamed only by the caressing touch of intercourse.
In short, the places of the body that
Others do not often touch have heightened sensation.

259. Where there is heat, it's moist, and hair grows.
All these areas of the body are doors to passion.
These nine places should be bitten, it's said.
These nine places should be rubbed and sucked, it's said.
Your own mind will show you what is right.

260. Also, because each day the essential elements
Move to different places of the body,
If you kiss those places at those times,
It is said that sexual passion will vastly increase.

261. They say that from dawn until midnight on the sixteenth day
The essence of semen resides in the crown of the head.
Likewise on the seventeenth it is at the ears,
And during the day on the eighteenth it is at the nose.

262. Then to the mouth, the cheeks, and the shoulders,
The chest, the belly, the navel, the buttocks, and the genitals,
The thighs, the knees, the calves, the ankles;
From the nineteenth to the new moon.

263. Then, on the first day, back to the calves,
On the second to the knees, on the third to the thighs.
It moves to the other parts in reverse order.
On the fifteenth it pervades the entire body.

264. First kiss the arms and then under the arms,
Then slowly kiss the belly.
Becoming more intoxicated, kiss the thighs and *bhaga*.
In this way draw the streams of rivers into the sea.

Four

TYPES OF BITES [AND SCRATCHES]

265. Indulging in small talk, joking, laughing, fighting, [33]
Slapping each other, strong bites and scratches,
Taking turns on top;
The passion of sex is called the battle of men and women.

266. Drunkenly grabbing with teeth and hands,
Roughly playing, seeking a chance to couple;
These deeds that occur in a state of passion
Are also done by wild beasts in the forest.

267. Starting with smiles and heaving sighs,
He holds her waist with his hand
And makes small pinches like grains of rice on her breast.
This is called *ācchurita* or scratch-like.

268. Licking from the mouth of the *bhaga* to the navel,
And dragging with the back of one's thumbnail,

This causes great itching in the woman.
This is called *dīrgarekha* or long drawing.

269. With a face red and boiling with the blood of passion
He hugs her chest and breasts as if to smash them.
They drag their nails down each other's backs.
This is called [leaving the] *tracks of the tiger*.

270. Squeezing the *liṅga* in the palm of her hand,
She presses [the head] with her thumb and, with the other four fingers
Wrapped around, she presses up and down to the base.
This is known as the *maṇḍala* or circle.

271. Grabbing the thighs and breasts with his fingers,
He scratches hard with four [fingernails],
And sometimes drags his fingers down the spine.
This is called the *shape of a half moon*.

272. Squeezing the tip of her breast and the mouth of her vagina, [34]
He pinches her hard by digging his thumbnail,
Leaving a cluster of pinch marks in their place.
This is known as the *footprint of the peacock*.

273. Drunk with passion, pinching the back and the buttocks
With four fingers over and over,
This is the track of the jumping rabbit.
It's done in quick succession, one after another.

274. Pinching the shoulders, chest, and belly
With all five fingernails,

Leaving deep red scratches.
This is called *lotus petals*.

275. Making scratches, deep and very red,
On the thighs, buttocks, and breasts;
Feeling with open fingers, without wounding,
The armpits, head, *liṅga*, and *bhaga*.

276. It is said that it is sometimes fitting
To wound the upper arms, neck, and back of the shoulders.
Until the wounds are healed, leaving no scar,
The enjoyment of passion will not be forgotten, it's said.

277. To end the limpness of the marvelous male member,
To excite the mind and make the body itch,
To display the strength of inner passion,
These are the purpose of pinching.

278. When the lovers part later, if they pinch each other strongly
On the shoulder and on the top of the head,
It will serve as a cause to remember and not forget.
The vermillion on a woman's head is such a mark, they say.

279. Pinch the throat and shoulders at the time of meeting.
Pinch the breasts at the point of entering the *bhaga*.
Pinch the back and waist at the time of intercourse.
Dig [the fingers] into the spine at the time of emission.

280. As long as she remains naked and free of shyness,
As long as her neck is arched and she is moist with wetness,
As long as he is at the point of coming,
So long should he engage in biting and scratching.

281. When he is close to climax,
She should pinch the tops of his ears,
Making semen come out for an instant. [35]
Sometimes it helps to pinch the armpit.

282. Once grown accustomed to scratching,
One cannot have satisfying sex without it.
In many lands, passionate women
Crave the touch of the nails.
To have sex without biting and pinching
Is like having sex without kissing.

283. When they first meet and passion is growing
Or when the time of intercourse approaches,
He should press her, push her, slap her,
Pull her hair, and bite her.

284. Shaking her body, with moaning sounds,
He kisses the nape of her neck,
Gently squeezing her lip between his teeth.
This is *guḍaka*, drops.

285. Kissing hard and touching teeth to teeth,
Strongly lock the lips with the teeth.
Forming a swelling as its trace.
This is called *ucchunaka*, swelling.

286. Face to face and speaking words of passion,
Two small teeth marks are made
From the lower lip to the chin.
This is called *drops of ambrosia*.

287. Then, making bite marks with all the teeth
On the two cheeks and the arms,
Forming a garland of red spots.
This is called *jewels of coral.*

288. After pressing the naked woman down on a cushion
And looking at her, top and bottom,
Biting all the fleshy parts of her body.
This is called *bindumāla*, garland of dots.

289. Drunk, the longing more and more unbearable,
Make rows of bites, one above the other,
On the breasts and the soft part of thighs.
This is called *fragments of clouds.*

290. Mouth joined to mouth, strongly sucking the tongue and lips, [36]
Drawing them between the teeth,
Then pulling them in at just the right amount.
This is called *puṣpakeśa*, flower's anther.

291. Thus with strong passion rising, placing the mouth
On the cheek, armpits, and places below the navel,
Pressing them with the teeth and drawing them upward.
This is known as *root of the willow.*

292. All fitting expressions of beauty and smiles,
Switching back and forth like magical illusions,
With a laughing face, blazing with a blood red glow;
This is called the great Frightful Goddess, pouch of passion.

Five

DESCRIBING THE MODES OF PLEASURE

293. Scratches on a young girl's breasts,
A woman's bite marks on a man's body;
Seeing these, even the mind of a queen suddenly wanders
And her expression changes.

294. Her body covered with deep scratches,
Her lips bloodied by a young man's savage passion;
Such a female messenger
Betrayed her queen, they say.

295. It is said that flowers, fruit, molasses, and things
Ruined by bite marks and scratches,
When sent by a man to a woman,
The power of passion steals her mind.

296. Drawing pictures of animals mating
On the leaves of a *nandakara* tree

And showing it cunningly in a secluded place,
A princess was won over once, it's said.

297. Making a mark resembling a bite mark
Below the lower lips of women
Is still seen in some regions of India. [37]
Whatever arouses passion is a woman's ornament, they say.

298. This passion that arises so naturally
In all men and women without effort
Is covered by a thin veil of shame.
With just a little effort, it shows its true face, naked.

299. Look at a picture of a naked couple making love,
Watch horses and cattle mating,
Write and read treatises on passion,
Talk about the types of passion.

300. Even for a man whose youth has passed,
As long as his passion has not grown weak,
His channels and semen remain warm,
So the force of his body, inside and outside, does not decline.

301. Spontaneous bliss is uncontrived and self-arisen,
Yet the entire world wears a mask of artifice.
Thus, at the time of delight
A man and woman must shun all customs and facade.

302. Who divided the upper and lower parts into clean and
dirty?
What determines the top and bottom of the body as good
and bad?

Showing off the upper half and hiding the lower half,
This is a civilized practice without wonder.

303. The hills and valleys of a place add to its beauty.
The thorns of thought are the roots of illness.
To stop thought without meditation,
For the common person, comes only in the bliss of sex.

bāhumūlakucadvandvayonisparśanadarśanāt
kasya na skhalati cittam retaḥ skannaṃ ca no bhavet[1]

304. Seeing and caressing the arms,
Breasts, and the female mark,
There is none whose mind does not weaken
And whose juices do not drip.

susnigdharomarahitaṃ pakvāśvatthadalākṛtiṃ
darśayiṣyāmi tat sthānaṃ kāmamegehaṃ sugandhikaṃ

305. Free of hair, its waters soft, moist, and boiling,
The house of passion with its fragrant scent,
Its shape resembles a full-grown leaf of the Bodhi tree; [38]
In its presence I will reveal myself.

| (These two verses are taken from the *Padmapurāṇa*.)

306. As a man becomes lustful,
So a skilled woman should
Touch him playfully, reveal her breasts,
And befuddle him with talk of passion.

1. Here and in the next stanza, Gendun Chopel is translating from the *Padmapurāṇa* (Pāṭālakhaṇḍa, chap. 106, verses 17 and 22) and provides the Sanskrit for each.

307. Moaning again and again she should kiss him,
Extending her chest and lower body toward him, she should embrace him.
Intoxicated herself, with intoxicating postures,
Completely unclothed, she takes the form of a naked woman.

308. Then, abandoning all notions of shame,
With a lustful look of flaming passion,
She should gaze at the erect *liṅga*.
Caress it, stroke it, rub and squeeze it.

309. Alas, the Lord of Pleasure has bestowed
The path of life to the women of this world.
So sustain this life force of desire, stable and firm,
This whirlpool of passion with its waves of longing.

310. The small vessel filled with flesh in the lower part
Of a naked young woman in the prime of her life,
Born to bestow the feast of pleasure,
There resides the essence of the joy of all joys.

311. The flower of falsehood has fallen behind the ear.
The strings of doubt have been fed to mice.
The fish of shame has been carried off by a black crow.
No one exists; just this [sexual bliss] is here.

312. On the bow of flowers the arrow of desire is undrawn,
Its jewel tip filled with the milk of ambrosia,
Seeing this shiny thing with a red color of coral,
Even the daughters of the gods come falling to the ground.

313. Just touching with the tip is the taste of milk.
To enter inside is delicious molasses itself.

To churn and thrust is sweet honey.
Grant me these distinct delicious tastes, sweet and flavorful.

314. Raised in the front like the shell of a tortoise,
Its entrance is covered by layers of soft flesh. [39]
This lotus door is intoxicating and burns with the heat of pleasure.
See this smile, made of dewdrops of desire.

315. It's not a flower with a thousand or a hundred petals;
It is a mound of sweetness endowed with dewdrops of desire.
In it is the taste of self-arisen honey,
The refined essence of joining the two, white and red.

316. A shiny black braid hangs beside her neck.
A jeweled loincloth is tied around her waist.
She uses anklets as earrings.
Be attuned to your partner's movements.

317. Her soft breasts swaying on her beautiful chest,
Her youthful body, with firm round arms unfolded,
Her lower body voluptuous with abundant flesh,
The body of a woman is a mass of honey.

318. Seeing the lotus of intoxicating ambrosia
Between the stout banana trees of her thighs,
Plunge into the woman, a marsh of desire,
Like a bull in the springtime.

319. Pressing against the chest of a passionate woman,
Her curving waist moving like a fish,
Swimming in the ocean of passion,
Even the atoms of your body become blissful.

Six

PLAYING WITH THE ORGAN

320. Entering with anxious haste right after meeting,
And losing the juices right after entering,
This is the way a dog swallows lungs.[1]
Not even the slightest pleasure is found in this.

321. Those who wish the fire of passion to blaze supreme
Should enter the place of passion's rite.
Arrange the bed for the purposes of pleasure,
Where the beautiful fireboard sits.[2] [40]

322. Putting her right leg on his shoulder,
She reveals her breasts and *bhaga*.

1. This is an allusion to the Tibetan expression "a dog finding a piece of lung" (*khyi dang glo pa phrad pa*), "lung" referring to the Tibetan delicacy of a marinated lung fried in oil. Although this is a delicacy, if a dog finds it, it will gobble it down without savoring it.

2. The imagery is from Vedic fire sacrifice, where the priest uses a wooden drill. The woman here is the fireboard where the priest rotates the drill to spark the flame.

With the palm of her moist hand
She strikes the center of her vagina.

323. She then plays all the games of heightened passion
With his flower, the organ of complete pleasure,
Which, like the dagger of a sorcerer,
Is always concealed in various ways.

324. Embracing the neck of her lord firmly with her left hand
She kisses him again and again.
Stretching out her right hand, she grasps the shaft of the *liṅga*
And milks it like the udder of a cow.

325. Rolling it between her two palms,
She pulls it just enough, twisting it right and left.
Shaking it back and forth, and holding it from the root,
She strikes her thighs, lips, and teeth with it.

326. When his *liṅga* has become erect,
She squeezes and rubs it between their bellies.
Sometimes holding it between her thighs,
She rubs the entrance of her *bhaga*.

327. Placing the *liṅga* between her fingers,
She looks at it with eyes of heightened passion.
Holding the testicles in her hand,
She rubs the large veins of the penis again and again.

328. Caressing his buttocks with her hand,
She pulls the tip of his penis and rubs
The places where the itch of passion rises:
The navel, throat, and sides of the breasts.

329. She touches the hole where the seed emerges
With her nipples and tips of her fingers.
When he is especially intoxicated with stirrings of passion,
She digs into the hole with her tongue and sucks.

330. With her fingernails, she makes it itch around the base
And massages the soft jewel with her hand.
She places it into the mouth of the *bhaga* again and again, [41]
Inserting it halfway in and then pulling it out.

331. Because it brings excellent lineage and the glories of pleasure,
Because it is the life force and the essence of innate divinity,
To prevent any intoxicating deeds
At the time of pleasure is said to be a sin.

332. When the force of the woman's passion
Is more powerful than the man's, if they make love,
The strength of pleasure is sustained.
If pregnancy results, it will surely be a son.

333. The woman who enhances the self-arisen *liṅga*
With the petals of her mouth
Will delight the great god Śiva,
Gaining glory, wealth, and supreme sons.

Seven

MOUNTING AND THRUSTING

334. Both hearts pounding with passion,
They gaze at each other, their faces flushed and fearless.
Leading the jewel of the organ with her hand,
She places it inside her *bhaga*.

335. Putting in just the tip, she takes it out again.
Putting it halfway in, she takes it out again.
Finally, pushed down to its root,
It points upward for a long time.

336. Bending her legs back,
She strikes his buttocks.
Her knees touching his armpits,
Her thighs and calves bind him, rubbing down.

337. Whenever the *liṅga* comes out,
She holds it in her hand, stroking it,
Then lets go, sending it slowly inside again,
One, two, three fingerbreadths deep.

338. When it has disappeared inside [42]
She gently caresses the testicles.
Squeezing the *liṅga*'s base with two fingers,
She stirs it inside her *bhaga*.

339. After two or three strokes,
She wipes the tip with soft silk,
Making it very thick and hard.
She also wipes the opening of her *bhaga*.

340. Always keeping the base moist,
She wipes the tip and shaft again and again.
Women who seek the power of pleasure
Should learn this secret instruction.

341. Then, with the longing for sex burning bright,
Their arms entwined, he goes below.
From one end to the other of their broad bed,
They roll back and forth, making love.

342. As they long, they weep.
As they remember, they speak.
When they have scaled all the walls of shame,
Their pleasure has great power.

343. Performing in every way
Their favorite postures of passion,
They come to know all the pleasures
Set forth in the treatises.

344. Close, trusting, free of worry,
When both are drunk with deep desire,
What would they not do when making love?
They do everything; they leave nothing.

345. Not right for a third person to see,
Not right for a fifth ear to hear,
Those who share such special secrets
Become best heart-friends in the world.

346. Thus, being led to the path of total intoxication
By various magical manifestations of passion,
The two kinds of women—the hard and the dripping—
Proceed down the path of pleasure as they wish.

347. Her body and mind unchanging and her passion difficult to rise, [43]
This type is known as the hard woman.
Her expression quickly changing and moist with fluids,
She is known as the dripping woman.

348. If he copulates quickly,
She will not be satisfied the first time.
Those with great strength and much semen,
Must make love two or three times.

349. Or, at the point when the semen is about to come,
He can stop thrusting and spread out the pleasure.
Then, arousing his passion again, he can resume.
Regardless, one needs to make love twice, it's said.

350. Just after the semen is emitted, the male member
Should not be taken out but kept deep inside the *bhaga*.
Let her do what she wishes
To complete her pleasure through shaking and moving.

351. If her pleasure is still not complete,
Place two fingers inside the *bhaga* and churn.

Churning and rubbing the hole of the *bhaga*
Prior to intercourse is key.

352. Also, repeatedly churning inside the vagina
With a wooden male member at the outset
And mounting the woman when she is drunk [with passion],
This is still the custom in southern regions.

353. When their husbands are away,
Women do it themselves.
It's said the rich even have them made for that purpose,
Of precious metals like gold, silver, and copper.

354. Most women in the land of India
Know their own husbands alone.
Since fulfilling sex is rare,
There are many such secret practices.

355. Even the retinue of queens, guarded by eunuchs,
Always rely on [practices like] this.
In our scriptures such tales occasionally appear,
But in the *Kāmasūtra* this is offered as an instruction. [44]

356. It's said that a woman married to a quick man for three years
Does not experience the pleasure of sex even once.
For men who do not know the inner experience of their partner,
This would be a good reason to become a monk.

357. Without creating strong thoughts of passion in a woman
Through the various practices,
One does not engage in the actual act of intercourse.
This, in brief, is the essential message of all the treatises on
passion.

358. The small fleshy lump at the secret entrance becomes erect.
She shakes, throbs, becomes chatty, burns with heat, and her fluids flow.
Her face becomes red, her eyes do not waver.
These are said to be the signs that a woman is very intoxicated.

359. For a woman who is not ensnared in passion,
To forcibly urge her and have intercourse against her will,
This is a mound of sin and the custom of the uncivilized.
If pregnancy results only a girl will come.

360. However, this race of women is very shy.
They are hard to convince with talk of passion.
If they are frightened by the sound of raised voices,
It is always difficult for the deeds of a man to be done.

361. A man and woman just smiling at each other,
If you think about it, has the meaning of sex.
Without being caught in choosing between good and bad,
Engage in sex whenever suitable, with whomever you can find.

362. Not because of renunciation, not because of religion,
Not because it is the right way, not because of a vow,
The one who still binds himself with chains [of celibacy],
Such an innocent man is just wasting his human life.

363. There are passionate people who wear a disguise,
Trying to suppress [their passion] in so many ways.
The kind of deeds they do in secret are said to be
Axes that chip away at their body's vital force.

364. She lies on her back with the soles of her feet together
And he binds them with his hands,

Then lifts her from her buttocks on his lap and enters.
This is called the *karkaṭaka* or crab. [45]

365. Sometimes flapping her knees like the ears of an elephant,
She beats them against the sides of his ribs.
She lies on her back with her legs crossed;
He remains below her and enters her as before.

366. Sometimes he binds her ankles with a scarf;
Sometimes she herself holds them together.
She lies on her back and places her buttocks before him
With her knees drawn up and her two thighs opened.

367. With their mouths joined they make love;
This is called the easy way to enter.
It is done almost everywhere in the world.
This is known as the *supine cowherdess*.

368. She kneels with her thighs open
And grasps his shoulders with her hands.
He also kneels and with his hands
He squeezes her breasts.

369. They leave a wide space between their upper bodies.
This is called the fully open *utphullaka*.
He gazes at her breasts and *bhaga*.

370. His thigh is placed between her thighs
And he hugs one of her thighs.
With their legs stretched out, they join together.
This is called *indrāṇikā*, Indra's woman.

371. Placing her below, he copulates from above.
She rides on top of him and copulates.
Likewise, they copulate lying side by side.
Sometimes, he copulates from behind.

372. They copulate squatting and they copulate standing.
Intertwined, with head and foot reversed, they copulate.
Hanging her in the air
With a rope of silk, they copulate.

373. From these eight main types of intercourse,
In the secrecy of home, whatever they desire unfolds.
Those that might damage the veins, bones, or flesh
Should not be done suddenly without familiarity and practice. [46]

374. She lies on her back with her thighs spread open.
He places a cushion under her buttocks and raises her *bhaga*.
She places her two feet on his spine.
They firmly join down to the root of the penis.

375. Holding her with his hands, he pulls her down.
Bracing her feet against the wall, he thrusts upward.
Pulling out, he emerges to the tip.
Pushing in, he brings it in to the root of the penis.

376. Their mouths joined, their chests rubbing together,
Her hands grasp his buttocks.
Sometimes he rubs her breasts.
Sometimes she caresses his testicles.
This is the ultimate sweetness for the passionate.
It is known as *guḍodaka*, juice of molasses.

377. He holds her well under her knees
And lifts her upward.
She holds him around the neck
And arches her head and upper body backward,
With only her buttocks resting on his penis.
She acts as if she were on a swing.

378. Sometimes he bends down onto a chair.
Sometimes he sits cross-legged.
If he is strong, it is appropriate to even walk around.

379. These can be done with the aid of suspending ropes,
A method that can be used in many situations.
She opens her thighs and forcefully stretches out her legs;
She mounts him like a horse and copulates.

380. Pressing hard on the sides of her thighs,
He might place a pillow on her buttocks.
This is called *sāratā* or powerful.
Most marvelous and offering the flavors of pleasure,
All the passionate like this.

381. Lying on her back,
She points her soles on the right and left of his waist.
She rubs him deeply and lifts him up.
This is called *preṅkha* or pushing. [47]

382. She wraps one leg around his waist
And puts the other on his shoulder or his head.
This is called *tassels of grain.*
It is a firm union, bestowing pangs of passion.

383. Both standing or kneeling, they copulate.
They copulate with their upper bodies arched backwards,
Their fingers just touching the ground from behind.
This is strongly pressing down, *pataka*.

384. Standing, the male and female marks join together.
They turn forward and backward and copulate.
Sometimes she leans her back against the wall.
This is known as *standing copulation*.

385. She sits on a chair,
Placing both feet on his shoulders.
From the front, he spreads her thighs and they copulate.
The roots of the male and female marks meet.
Therefore, this is called *nothing in between*.
It especially satisfies the passionate woman.

386. A variation: when copulating in this way,
Her two ankles are tied to a rope
And he carries them on his back.
If uncomfortable, he puts the rope below his arms or back.

387. Another variation: at that time,
He holds her legs,
Opening them wide with his hands.
By your experience you'll know it is most pleasurable.

388. Seated cross-legged and arching slightly backward,
He opens her thighs on his lap and keeps them there.
Embracing his shoulders or arms with her hands,
She places her two feet on the ground, behind him.

389. This is called *enjoyment*.
The act of going in and out is done just by the woman.
For many, this moving swing is most pleasurable. [48]

390. Another variation: place a small but slightly high cushion
Under the buttocks of the squatting woman;
His heels touch the base of his buttocks.

391. With the sides of his thighs, he spreads her legs back.
He places her buttocks on his penis and joins.
Here, going in and out is done by him.
It is said to bestow the enjoyment of supreme pleasure.

392. Tightly joining the mouth of the *bhaga*
With the root of the *liṅga* without moving in and out,
He sways his upper body to the right and left
Like a moving swing hanging from a solid branch.

393. With the tip of his penis touching the depth of the *bhaga*,
This is called the *motion of the swing*.
Many women take delight in this.
She should do this in accord with her experience.

394. Whether done by the man or by both,
This act of going in and coming out,
This well-known way is called the *motion of the pestle*.
Taking it out just halfway,
Sometimes withdrawing it sideways.

395. Just as a bee grasps the anther of a lotus
And rapidly shakes its lower part of the body,
Likewise shake her buttocks in a circular motion.
This is called the *wheel* and the *sound of a bee*.

396. It's not tiring, not disheartening, does not sap the strength of the body,
And your pleasure does not culminate for a long time.
If you are able to bear the pangs of passion,
Engaging in this motion of the swing is key.

397. For someone who is not satisfied by just shaking and churning,
Though there is no guarantee that this will bring satisfaction,
Because this can scratch the places that itch inside,
This secret method brings delight to many women.

398. This [male] organ is an external appendage.
That [vagina] is a hole inside a body.
Since naked flesh and sinew are different,
How can a thorn sense what the wound feels?

399. Opening wide her binding thighs in front, [49]
He presses his weight against the junction of the pelvic bones,
And he places the tip of burning red coral jewel deep inside.
There he performs the ritual of female joy.

400. With both organs tightly bound,
He moves his buttocks right and left,
With his *liṅga* stirring deep inside the *bhaga*, like churning butter.
This is called *manthana*, the churning.

401. Sometimes holding the root of his *liṅga* in his hand
He shakes it inside the *bhaga*.
This is a medicine that cures the pain of passion.
It should be done for dripping women.

402. Entering right away, at the end of the first thrust
He thrusts upward, one, two, three, four times.
Again, he enters two or three times.
This is the soaring movement of a bird.

403. With her thighs together she extends her legs out
And mounting him like a frog,
She strikes the *liṅga* hard like driving a stake.
This is called very forceful, *hula*.
This should be done by hard women.

404. Just as a plough breaks the soil,
By raising and lowering his hips,
His *liṅga* hits the *bhaga* up and down.
This is called *siṭitaka*, torment.

405. Like pushing a boulder with one's back,
They join the mouth of the *bhaga* and the root of the penis.
Pressing strongly, they copulate for a long time.
This is called *intoxicating copulation*.

406. Just as a bull and cow copulate,
He enters the *bhaga* to the right and left.
Thrusting inside, he moves the tip upward,
While the lower parts of their bodies strike each other.
This is called *vṛṣa*, the copulation of the bull.

407. Just as a stallion and a mare copulate,
Drawing his *liṅga* far outside, with a swooshing sound,
He inserts it to up to the root. [50]
He strikes and she responds.
This is called *aśva*, the copulation of horses.

408. Just as a male and female boar copulate,
Slowly, slowly he inserts his penis upward.
As it arrives at the root, he pushes and thrusts fiercely,
With the tip almost touching the entrance of the womb.
This is called the copulation of the *varāha*.

409. Then, when they are both tired,
They rest, forehead touching forehead.
Then, once again, in the order described above,
They play the games of joy until they are satisfied.

410. The clouds of old hopes and fears fade into the sky.
The moon of self-arisen elements melts into milk.
The great bliss of space, clear and free of conceptions,
Offer this gift to blossoming young girls.

Eight

MOANS

411. If they are struck in the places of passion,
Women will instantly make a gasping sound, as if afraid.
Like when one's chest is hit with cold water,
They exhale rapid breaths as if counting them.

412. Sometimes it is the wordless groans of a mute.
Sometimes it is a clearly spoken babble.
As passion rises higher and higher,
There are the surprising calls of eight birds.

413. As her lower body aches with pangs of passion,
She embraces her man and places her mouth to his.
From deep inside her throat she makes the sound *ooh*.
This experience is known as the *call of the dove*.

414. With the tip of the jewel deep inside her,
Touching the entrance of the womb, and with spark-like
passion,

She emits the sound *huh*, the call of the *kokila* (the Tibetan cuckoo).
The call of this bird sounds choked, subtle, and striking.

415. Tormented by unbearable passion, [51]
She lets out an unclear *dutkṛta*.
This is the *call of the peacock*, like echoes in a ravine.
The call of this bird is like the sound of a cat.

416. Swooning in the sleep of ineffable bliss,
She dreams of the heavens making love to the earth.
With spontaneous chatter she releases all sorts of moans.
This is the melodious hum of the bee sipping honey.

417. When the skin of shyness is pierced
By the sharp needle of unbearable passion,
To forcefully pierce further she utters, *śāta artha*.
This sound of a bell is known as the *call of a goose*.

418. When the root of the *liṅga* enters the lotus,
Completely intoxicated, she babbles madly,
Saying *mokṣārtha* for the sake of her release.
This is known as the call of the *lāvaka*.

419. With the touch of organs joined with no space between,
She yearns for the taste of insatiable passion.
She shouts *a ma ma artha* so that he may thrust.
This is called the *song of the black goose*.

420. Because of intense pleasure, he thrusts forcefully.
At each stroke of entry and exit, she says *paramārtha*.
This sound is the call of the swallow.
Breaking through every corner and boundary, it resounds.

421. Penetrated with savage power, she is satisfied.
Though tormented by the fire of passion, her pleasure burns.
Though she weeps with unbearable moans, her joy increases.
Great indeed is the nature of this wondrous bliss.

Nine

ACTS OF A MAN [DONE BY A WOMAN]

422. Placing her two feet under his armpits,
She mounts him facing backwards.
Bending down, she leans against his ankles, [52]
Holding them with her right and left hands.

423. Then, she moves her buttocks forward and backward.
Pulling the *liṅga* upward, she places it inside her.
She presses it hard, as if it were a stick,
Around her *bhaga*, left, right, front, and back.
This gives joy to a young man with a hard *liṅga*
And to a passionate woman.

424. On a sofa the length of the body
Or on a pile of long and narrow cushions,
He lies on his back.
She mounts as before, turning front to back.

425. She places the *liṅga* inside the *bhaga*
And places her right and left feet on the floor.

She rotates her hips as before.
Sometimes she switches to the front and mounts [as before].

426. With both of them kneeling on the bed,
Her left thigh is pressed by his [right] thigh;
His left thigh is pressed by her [right].
The lower parts of both of their bodies slightly slanted,
they join.

427. They embrace each other with their upper legs.
Sometimes they switch positions of their thighs.
Using this technique of crossing copulation,
Other standing and lying postures can be adopted as well.

428. Placing his buttocks on a chair,
With the soles of his feet on the floor,
She raises herself onto his lap and they embrace.
She places her legs behind him.

429. Holding her waist with his hands,
He raises her up and presses her down.
Sometimes, by rotating her pelvis,
Without going in and out, she gently churns the *bhaga*.

430. A passionate woman of the land of Persia
Can only be satisfied by this method of copulation.
It is called the *fragrant garden*;
In the Arabic language, it is known as *kelakara*. [53]

431. For men who are weak, tired, or fat
And for women who are especially passionate,
Performing the deed of mounting the man
Is known as the woman doing the man's work.

432. In India old men take young wives
But can barely carry the burden of their belly.
For the most part, they follow this practice.
In many lands, this is a common custom.

433. He lies on his back with his thighs spread and his legs stretched out.
She lies down on top, her calves together,
And places [her *bhaga*] on the root [of the penis], her thighs and *bhaga* closed.
Holding his shoulders with her hands,
She rotates her pelvis and strongly grinds.
This is known as the *way of the mare*.

434. In that posture or mounted on top like a horse,
The mouth of the *bhaga* and the root of the male member touch.
Leaning their lower bodies against each other, they embrace.
In this, the in-and-out motion is not done.

435. Then, alternating right and left, up and down,
She rotates her pelvis back and forth.
This is *bhramaraka*, bee.
It is known as the way that a bee extracts honey.

436. The tip of the *liṅga*, like the hole in a millstone,
Stirs and turns deep in the *bhaga*.
Lying on his back, he inserts the penis
And stretches her two feet on his chest.
Joining hands, they make the motion of a swing.
This is called *being in a boat*.

437. Lying on his back with her on top,
She places her hands and feet on the ground, bends down, and mounts him.

With each withdrawal and entry she examines his thick and long [penis],
Watching it go inside her.
This practice of intoxicated women
Is called *gatāgata*, going and coming.

438. She sits on his penis,
Stretching her legs until they are under his armpits.
Putting her hands on the ground on the right and left, [54]
They do whatever is pleasurable: the movements of the pestle or the swing.
This is called the *melody of the palanquin.*

439. Lying on his back, his upper body leaning on a pillow,
She places her legs behind his back.
Their chests touching, she embraces his shoulders.
This is called *rodhanika*, reverse method.
The way of the pestle and swing are both done.

440. With the [organs] well-joined, his legs
Embrace her spine, as a woman does.
This is known as *holding the small pouch.*
Because the in-and-out motion is difficult, they use the movement of the swing.
For other wondrous methods of copulation as well,
This way of the swing is utter pleasure.

441. He lies on his back with his thighs open
And keeps both his knees sharply bent upwards.
She places her buttocks on the penis
And puts her feet on either side of him.

442. Leaning back on his thighs,
She performs the in-and-out motion.

By this method, the *liṅga* enters deeply,
Even touching the door of the womb again and again.

443. Therefore, it is prohibited for the pregnant.
This is called *rodhanika*, reverse method.
A man has a little of woman's nature
And a woman has a little of man's nature.

444. When a woman mounts a man, a fierce expression can appear
On her face that he has never seen before.
However, a man and woman who are seeking a child
And wishing for pregnancy should shun this method.

445. The young, drunk with passion, use these
Modes of copulation, changing positions above and below.
They say that in Malaya, women are accustomed to this method.
Even when bribed with gold, they will not lie on the bottom.

Ten

VARIOUS METHODS OF COPULATION

446. He lifts her on his lap from her back.
Stretching her pelvis outward, she joins him at her buttocks.
With one hand he holds her breast;
With the other he squeezes the *bhaga* from the side.

447. Bound together just right, he exits and enters her slowly.
Sometimes she braces her hand against the wall.
While performing this type of intercourse,
With his finger he strokes the little piece of flesh above the *bhaga*.
If he slowly strokes below her cheeks and her thighs,
This will produce immeasurable pleasure.

448. She lies on her side and pushes the top of her buttocks backward.
He lies behind her and meets her *bhaga*.
He places his head under her arm,
Kissing and rubbing the top of her breasts.

449. He sits on a chair and leans back.
She thrusts her buttocks to the side and they meet.
She lifts both legs to the left, over his thigh.
With one hand he embraces her neck.

450. She lies on her back with a cushion under her buttocks.
Her two feet are drawn into the air with a rope.
He grasps her knees from the front and enters.
Leaving her in that same position
For a short time after the union
Is said to help conception.

451. He sits on a chair and leans back,
With both feet firmly on the floor in front.
With his thighs spread, he places his buttocks on the edge of the seat.
She moves onto his lap with her back.
Stretching her buttocks outward, the *liṅga* enters the *bhaga*.

452. She braces her two feet against the base of the wall
And thrusts her *bhaga* strongly against his penis.
Rubbing and turning with her buttocks, [56]
Sometimes bracing her hands against a ladder in front,
She withdraws and enters.

453. Or, bracing her hands against a bar,
She presses down to the root of the *liṅga* as before.
Changing the various heights of chairs, they copulate,
With the woman doing most of the moving and thrusting.

454. She kneels, leaning on the mattress.
She bends her waist and stretches her pelvis out.

Opening his thighs, he copulates from behind.
This is called *dhenuka*, cow.
Reaching his hand around her leg,
He rubs the swelling of the *bhaga* again and again.

455. A variation: she stands, bending forward.
Her hands braced against the bed, leaning on her elbows,
She bends her waist and stretches her buttocks out.
For women afflicted with strong passion,
This is said to be the best of all methods of copulation.
In many lands this is a common practice.

456. Another variation: she places her knees on the ground,
Stretching the top of her buttocks as before.
She lies on a cushion that raises her upper body slightly.
The man and woman press against each other equally.
He embraces her chest with his hands,
Rubbing upward on her belly.

457. Placing her two hands behind her,
She lies on her back on the man, pointing her buttocks at him.
Meeting from behind, they perform the motion of the swing,
Bestowing the flavors of intoxicating joy.

458. From behind, he stretches his legs forward
Beneath her thighs.
Sometimes she turns her buttocks to the side,
Stretching out both legs to his left.

459. Also sometimes she turns them to the right.
This is a good way to prevent pregnancy.
All types of standing and seated copulation are also helpful. [57]

460. Placing her buttocks on a chair,
She puts her two feet on the ground and opens her legs.
Lifting the upper part of her body,
Standing up, he copulates from the front.

461. This and other similar methods of copulation
Are very helpful in preventing pregnancy.
In brief, all methods of copulation in which the vagina is pointed down,
The *liṅga* goes in from below,
And the woman's waist is not bent forward,
Are helpful for preventing pregnancy.

462. As soon as the semen has been emitted
She should stand up and stamp the ground with her feet
And wash her *bhaga* with warm water.
This is like a medicine for preventing pregnancy.

463. Placing a pillow under her belly,
She stretches out her arms and legs and lies face down on the carpet.
Spreading his thighs, he mounts her from behind.
He places his cheek in the middle of her spine.

464. Pulling her from the base of her thighs,
He brings her buttocks repeatedly to his penis and thrusts.
Sometimes, with the fingers of both hands,
He squeezes the banks of the *bhaga* and copulates.

465. This and other methods of copulation from behind
Can be changed in different ways.
Stretching her buttocks outward, she shakes,
Rubbing and massaging his sides.

466. Bending his head down,
He kisses her pelvis.
Sucking the side of her belly,
He drags his tongue under her arms and breasts.

467. Perform these various intoxicating acts
At times when you like to do them.
By playing from behind, one can rub the anther of the *bhaga*; touching it directly,
One is able to awaken her fully.
Able to be satisfied by the fierce joy of passion,
It especially bestows pleasure on the woman. [58]

468. These methods of copulation with entry from behind
Are very helpful for becoming pregnant.
It is said that boys conceived from this position
Are particularly noble.

469. The emerging essence made from one's own indestructible elements,
This honey-like taste born from one's own self-arisen body,
Experienced through the hundred thousand pores,
This is something not tasted even by the tongue of the gods in heaven.

470. An old man who has done everything might say anything.
Someone who does everything in secret might condemn everything.
Though there are many sensual pleasures in this Realm of Desire,
Can there be anything that surpasses a woman's vagina?

Eleven

UNCERTAIN DEEDS

471. The essence, with the heat of pleasure still burning,
Is the ambrosial life force of all that lives.
Swallowing just a portion of a drop, they say,
Is better than a hundred of the best medicines.

472. Placing pillows under his buttocks and head,
He lies on his back at the end of the bed.
She mounts him in the backwards way
So that he can stroke her cheeks and thighs.

473. Joined in that way,
And by sucking and moving his tongue,
He suddenly induces intense pleasure for a long time.
Whispering in her ear, this is called *mukhamaithuna*.

474. Another term is *spinning pleasure*.
[The pleasure] is two times, three times, ten times, many times
[greater].
(It is also called lifted on top, *auparisṭaka*.)

475. At the time of joy, Śiva and his consort [59]
Are actually present in the bodies of the man and woman.
It is said that such acts destroy the obstacles to one's life,
And one's power, beauty, and youth burn bright.

476. The perception of ugly objects and impurity ceases.
One is freed from all fear and timid thoughts.
Body, speech, and mind are purified of all artifice,
And one arrives at the island of supreme joy.

477. These days, Western women are very experienced.
In India in ancient times (such as during the Gupta dynasty), it was widely practiced.
Most of the ancient brahmin temples
Are filled with images of such acts.

478. By performing deeds [deemed] inappropriate,
The passion for passion increases.
For those of little experience who are bashful,
All the methods of excess are prohibited.

479. Whatever comes from a woman's body at the time of sex is pure.
This is stated in the ancient scriptures.
(Like a bird when flying, a dog at the time of the hunt, and calves when they are sucking . . .)

480. A brahmin can be said to drink beer from a woman's mouth
During sex until he is satisfied.
Otherwise, saying, "It comes from the blood of demigods,"
Even a taste of beer will destroy the lineage.

481. The *bhaga* of a passionate woman is the mouth of
Brahmā,
Bestowing body and bliss to the embodied.
Making love with another, one satisfies oneself.
This is the magic of Rāma, god of wealth, they say.

482. Binding the essence of a hundred thousand channels
Through the movement of the flaming tongues of passion;
For those intoxicated with unbearable joy,
Whatever there is, nothing is prohibited.

483. Copulating in front of a mirror,
Tormenting the nipples with the teeth and sucking them,
Bathing the dripping jewel with her tongue,
Intoxicated and confused, they will do anything.

484. Smearing each other with honey [60]
Or tasting each others' natural fluids
And sucking each other's small and thick swellings,
Intoxicated and confused, they will do anything.

485. Telling untoward tales,
Showing each other the secrets of their bodies,
Imagining wondrous places and making love,
Intoxicated and confused, they will do anything.

486. In the treatises of the ḍākinīs, it's said,
These kinds of sexual acts
Are to satisfy the extremely lustful men and women
Who can retain the essence in their body without
emission.

487. The self-arisen blood enters the man's body
And his lunar essence is absorbed into the woman's body.
Through this, like Śaṅkara and Umā,[1]
They are certain to attain power and supreme bliss.

1. This is a reference to the sexual union of the Hindu god Śiva and his consort Umā Devī, symbolized in the form of a *liṅga* standing erect from inside a *yoni* or *bhaga*.

Twelve

VARIOUS HELPFUL METHODS

488. For a strong man and passionate woman
Who freely enter the circle of pleasure
And wish to sustain their lovemaking in whatever way they desire,
The above are the ways of delight.

489. However, having understood well
The customs of various lands
And the differences among types of women, apply this
To the types of intercourse that are appropriate.

490. A woman who has just given birth or has a painful pregnancy,
Who is ill or is ridden with great worries,
Who is very old or very young,
Is never an appropriate object of desire.

491. Through playfulness and laughter in different ways,
Through lustful talk, rubbing, touching, kissing, [61]
Using whatever skillful method that is appropriate,
Tame those who are arrogant or bashful.

492. Cover a soft carpet with a white cloth.
Place vessels of fragrant liquids nearby.
Scatter bunches of flower petals.
Make beds to help calm the lotus type.

493. Cover a cushioned bed with multicolored cloth.
Arrange various paintings.
Place food and drink, such as honey, nearby.
Make beautiful beds for the painting type.

494. Cover the bed with soft and supple deerskin
Surrounded by many cushions of different sizes.
Place musical instruments there.
Make beds of wealth for the conch type.

495. Surround the edge of the bed in darkness.
Place a stiff carpet and hard pillows.
Arrange aphrodisiacs, like fish.
The elephant type play forcefully in bed.

496. In most women of the Aryan race,
Their *bhaga* is high toward their belly.
Pregnancy is difficult and painful.
Sexual methods from the front are appropriate.

497. In the women of the Mongol race,
Their belly is broad and the hole nearer to their buttocks.

Boys are easily born, even to very young women.
Sexual methods from behind are most suitable.

498. In women whose buttocks are thick,
Their *bhaga* is naturally higher.
Stretching her legs straight out on the rug,
He mounts her from the top and copulates.

499. In those whose belly is wide,
The *bhaga* is naturally lower.
Placing cushions under her buttocks,
He lifts her legs onto his shoulders and copulates.

500. The right and left sides have few folds. [62]
Free of hair, her hole is completely round.
Her anther is erect and a channel comes out at the top.
Such a lotus is known as the water-born.

501. The folds around the opening are thick and her cheeks are low.
With thick and tangled hair, her fluids are hot.
The inside of her lotus is narrow and grasps the tip of the *liṅga*.
Such a lotus is called the mud-born.

502. The entrance is tight and narrow, causing discomfort.
It burns hot and is rough like the tongue of a cow.
Her lotus has little fluid and makes the *liṅga* swell.
Such a lotus is called dry earth-born.

503. One who has red eyes and orange pupils,
Thick lips and an upper lip that curls upward,
And a space between her front teeth and red gums,
She is a passionate woman indeed.

504. The tip of her nose points down.
When she laughs, the veins on her forehead stand out.
With prominent cheekbones, the midpoint of her face protrudes.
Whenever these are seen, they are signs of being passionate.

505. Her eyes bulge and the veins on her face are red.
There are small wrinkles inside her ears.
Her hips and thighs are high and her calves are thick.
When these are seen, they are signs of great passion.

506. When looked at straight she fidgets.
When she talks, she repeatedly purses her lips.
There is a lotus pattern around her lips.
These are signs of great passion and an excellent *bhaga*.

507. In the first three days of menstruation,
A woman should be left alone in a solitary place.
On the fourth day, she washes her entire body
And rubs it well with fragrant oils.

508. If one has sex on these days,
It is a most unsuitable and vile deed.
If there is conception on the eleventh, thirteenth, or fifteenth day, [63]
Because it will be a girl, it should be avoided.

509. On the sixth, eighth, tenth, and twelfth day,
And also on the fourteenth day,
If she has sex and conceives,
The child will be a boy.

510. If conceived on the fifth day,
A girl will be born who achieves only average wealth.
If conceived on the sixth day,
A boy will be born who lives by base deeds.

511. If conceived on the seventh day,
A girl will be born with a religious mind and always happy.
If conceived on the eighth day,
A boy will be born who recites the various Vedas and
attains fame.

512. If conceived on the ninth day,
It will definitely be a girl, attractive like a *gandharva*.
By conceiving on the tenth day, brave boys will be born.
Victorious everywhere, they attain the glory of the dharma.

513. If conceived on the eleventh day,
A beautiful and intelligent girl will be born.
If conceived on the twelfth day,
It will be a boy with the power of youth, defeating his enemies.

514. On the thirteenth day, it will be a girl
With little lust or greed, respecting the dharma.
On the fourteenth, a boy will be born
Who will reap much fruit from his sinful deeds.

515. If conceived on the fifteenth day,
It will be a girl of pleasing form, but she will experience various
sufferings.
If conceived on the sixteenth day,
It will be a boy, learned and brave, gaining many types of
wealth.

516. The eighth and fourteenth of the month
As well as the full moon and new moon days
Are times for making offerings and performing rituals.
Because all the gods condemn it, avoid making love.

517. If a child is conceived at those times,
Evil and violent children will come. [64]
Likewise, if one has sex on the last day of the year
Or during an eclipse, it is said that the child will die.

518. In the second or third month after conception,
When she is free from pain after giving birth,
And a day has passed after menstruation,
A strong craving for sex arises in women.

519. If, while the man is nearby,
He does not make love to his wife at those times,
He abandons the practices of respectable men
And after he dies will go to a frightful hell.

520. These days for having sex
Are authorized by the ancient sages.
Many scholars say that most of the effects
Of the specific times are certain.

521. In particular, on the eighth day after menstruation has stopped,
Because the mouth of the womb is open, she will definitely conceive.
After that, although conception is possible,
For many women, the door of the womb closes.

522. Prior to making love, both the man and woman
Should remove any excrement and wash their genitals,
Especially cleaning the insides of the *bhaga*,
Thereby helping to keep the womb without faults.

523. At the time of union, if fear or panic arise,
A fault will later arise in the womb.
Therefore, it is of the greatest importance
To make love in a private place, relaxed and completely free from worry.

524. Then, as he closes his left nostril
And breathes through his right,
She lies down on her right side and he on his left.
After a little while, they fall asleep.

525. If they wish to have a male child,
The passion of the woman for the man must be strong.
He should try to make his passion weaker,
Such as imagining the woman in the form of a man.

526. If they wish to have a girl,
The passion of the man for the woman must be strong. [65]
The woman herself must remain indifferent,
And the man must strongly emit much semen.

527. This is an essential point of great importance;
Whether the child is male or female depends on this:
A passionate woman will have many sons.
If the man's passion is great, he is certain to have daughters.
Therefore, it is mistaken to think
That if his passion is powerful, he will have male children.

528. The mother's character, constituents, and physical strength
Will all go into the lineage of her sons.
In the same way, the father's character and physical constituents
Will definitely appear in the lineage of his daughters.

529. When the union is over, she should not stand up immediately,
But should lie on her back with a pillow under her buttocks.
Then, after drinking some milk,
It is good if they sleep separately in their own beds.

530. The first time they have sex,
The man's passion is naturally stronger.
Thus, at the time of emitting semen, he should withdraw the *liṅga*
And send his seed outside the *bhaga*.

531. The second time, because her passion is burning
He should send his seed inside the *bhaga*.
When she becomes pregnant, methods such as this
Definitely help a male child to appear.

532. When they are both drunk on powerful passion,
Because the power of the woman is naturally greater,
In most cases, the child will be born as a boy.
However, their [passion] must be equal before and after.

533. In short, until a powerful mind of passion has been produced in the woman
Through the various games of passion,
One should not have sex.
Among the most necessary essential points, this is beneficial.

534. Thinking that her insides are filled with filth,
Having no appetite,
And water and mucous dripping from the mouth,
These are said to be signs of pregnancy.
If she has a strong craving for sex, [66]
It is a sign that a daughter resides in her womb.

535. [Once pregnant,] always avoid conditions that create fear,
Such as looking into an abyss or down a well.
If she is able to avoid sex, that is good.
If she is not able, use methods of union lying on the side.

536. If the man presses down on the belly late in pregnancy,
It can damage the limbs of the child.
In particular, because the child's thumb is around its nose
There is great danger of causing a harelip.

537. At the time of childbirth, an experienced woman should be present.
She should gently push downward on the belly and squeeze.
Then the head appears at the door to the female mark.
By squeezing strongly, the child will come out easily.

538. If the door of the womb is blocked, fumigate with the skin of a black snake.
By stretching out the arms and shaking them, the afterbirth will come out.
Then, when menstruation appears again,
It is called the postpartum purging.

539. Although there are many sufferings difficult to endure,
No pleasure is more unbearable than this.

If the day of the full moon could be frozen,
No reason exists for darkness to appear until the new moon.[1]

540. If one does not know the methods for *holding* and *spreading*,[2]
The bliss that arrives at the tip of the jewel
Immediately disappears the instant you see it,
Like picking up a snowflake with one's hand.

541. Thus, when pleasure arises while churning,
Stop moving and allow it to spread again and again.
Again, using the above methods,
Pleasure can persist for a long time.

542. From time to time wipe both secret places
With a clean cloth.
Switch among the various types of methods of copulation.
By doing this, the pleasure will become very powerful.

1. In this somewhat oblique analogy, Gendun Chopel seems to be making the point that there exists an intimate link between our experience of pain and pleasure. The brightness of the full moon's light is relative to the pitch darkness of the night before the new moon, and pitch darkness of such a night is defined by its contrast to the night of a full moon. In the same manner, the intensity of the sexual pleasure and its unbearable nature is defined by its intimate connection with the experience of pain. If, by some method we were able to freeze the movement of the full moon day, it would prevent the appearance of the pitch darkness of the moonless nights. In the same manner, if a person has mastered some method of "holding off" ejaculation, he could prolong the experience of sexual bliss.

2. "Holding" (*'dzin pa*) and "spreading" (*bkram pa*) refer to techniques presented in the tantric texts for preventing ejaculation once the person has reached the point of orgasm. For example, in the *Vajramālā*, four methods of holding are mentioned: through mantra, through medicine, through special substances, and through wind yoga. In other texts, five such methods are listed: through special substances, yogic exercise, meditation, mantra, and wind yoga.

543. Hold the semen for a long time
By focusing the eye and mind
At a point in the middle of her brow and at her face
And strongly asking and answering with passionate words. [67]

544. When the seed has reached the root of the penis,
The lower part of his body becomes heavy and tight.
At that time, focus the mind on the expanse of space.
By forcefully drawing upwards, the flow will definitely reverse.[3]

545. Tighten the anus and turn your tongue and eyes upward.
Contract the joints of your arms and legs and strongly clench your fists.
Pull your belly inward to the spine and inhale.
These are the required yogic exercises.[4]

546. Focus the mind on numbers:
Eight times three is twenty-four, six times five is thirty.
So even if she pinches him and says, "Look here,"
And strongly urges him, he will be able to hold the semen.

547. When the entire body is pervaded by pleasure,
If he is able to stop the mind from going downwards
And experience the pleasure only in the upper part of the body,
He can play as long as he likes and the semen will not diminish.

548. Unable to experience pleasure completely pervading his body
In a manner that is broad and vast,

3. This verse presents the method of holding through meditation or visualization.

4. This verse presents the method of holding through yogic exercises.

But fixating his mind on the pleasure at the secret place alone,
This is a cause of losing the semen.

549. As they draw closer to the nature of things,
[Even] the words of the learned become mute.
Hence all phenomena, subtle by their very nature,
Are said to be beyond expression in words or thoughts.

550. In this saṃsāra, thick with the mirages of appearance,
Which [even] the Tathāgata's hand cannot stop,
The mind is placed in the nature of emptiness of all things.
Who can let go of belief in existence and nonexistence?

551. The child of awareness swoons in the sphere of passion.
The fickle intellect falls into a wormhole,
Being dragged down by lustful thoughts.
Behold, O being, the true nature of pleasure.

552. This wave of illusion, where the non-two appears as two,
Dividing into subject and object, [68]
Wishing to merge the ground of being with the ocean of bliss,
Do you not feel the motion and rising of the desire for sex?

553. Why would this reality, unsupported by magic, move about?
Where does this mind, with nothing pursuing it, run away to?
Because, abandoning their true nature, they are unable to stand still,
This couple, appearance and mind, move in the direction of bliss.

554. Each step we take is for the sake of pleasure.
Each word we speak is for the sake of pleasure.

Good deeds are done for the sake of pleasure.
Bad deeds are done for the sake of pleasure.

555. The eyeless ant runs for the sake of pleasure.
The legless worm crawls for the sake of pleasure.
In brief, all the world is racing with each other,
Running toward pleasure, one faster than the next.

556. The three billion worlds are suddenly swallowed
By a magnetic boulder, blind and senseless.
When one considers this, one will understand:
The sphere of great bliss is where all appearance and existence dissolve.

557. Not satisfied even with the wealth of three billion worlds,
The famous burn with covetous greed.
In reality, this mind, the clever mute child,
Seeks the space-like kingdom of bliss and emptiness.

> This easy-to-understand way of explaining how the two, bliss and emptiness, are combined in the manner of object and subject is very different from ideas in the tantras. Thus, here the meaning of the inexpressible final nature of the stable [environment] and the moving [world of beings] is this. They are said to be one, for when considered from the negative perspective, it is emptiness, and when it is perceived from the positive perspective, it is bliss. One might wonder, "Since emptiness is a non-affirming negative and bliss is a positive, how can it be possible for the two to be attributed to the same thing?" Do not be afraid of all such reasoning that is grounded in dualism.

558. To excellent beings, you display the true nature of reality.
To benighted children, you play tricks. [69]

Indefinable, you have defining characters.
I bow down to you, the god of self-arisen pleasure.

559. You appear to nonmeditators and to the mind of a fool.
You befriend all and all are your friend.
Seen by all, understood by none,
I bow down to you, god of self-arisen pleasure.

560. Sky dancer, unclothed by convention,
Magical forms, all without color or shape,
Casting the meteor of awareness, glimpsed but not grasped,
I bow down to you, god of self-arisen pleasure.

561. Where the rainbows of diverse elaborations dissolve,
Where the ocean of illusion is free from waves,
Where even the wavering mind does not waver,
I bow down to you, great self-arisen bliss.

562. The eyes of the Buddha see it without blinking.
The learned ones know it by ceasing to speak.
The ungrasping mind encounters it without concepts.
I bow down to you, the sphere of self-arisen bliss.

563. There is nothing here that involves divulging the secrets
Of tantra, such as its profound practices and terminology.
Still, this embarrassing practice
Is something we should try to keep secret from others.

564. For monks, arhats, elders, and self-enlightened ones,
This is not a text that they should be forced to read.
So instead of reading it and being ashamed and angry,
It would be better to just read the title and then set it aside.

565. This is a world of diverse dispositions.
Our thoughts and perceptions do not agree.
What some condemn, others praise.
What is clean for some, others judge dirty.

566. The meat-eating wolf and the grass-eating rabbit,
Rather than discussing what kind of food to eat,
It is best if they kept to their own ways,
Within the company of their own kind.

567. Making nomads eat pork, [70]
Making villagers drink melted butter,
It is useless to urge people to do what they don't like.
It is useless to stop them from doing what they like.

568. Good and bad, clean and dirty, these are just personal opinions,
And what one thinks goes on changing.
To keep arguing about it will just cause fatigue.
To search for reasons will just bring trouble.

569. From childhood to when we are old and decrepit,
Our attitudes change so many times.
Analyze your own experience and you'll know this.
What point is there in trusting today's thoughts?

570. Sometimes, seeing a goddess is revolting.
Sometimes, seeing an old woman creates lust.
We think, "This is the one," then someone else comes along.
How can one count the betrayals of the mind?

571. Having understood these well and become weary,
When the root of all perspectives is destroyed,

That is the great repose of bliss.
Another word for it is true liberation.

572. Lake Manasarovar, to those who have not seen it, is two miles wide.
When you reach it, it is a body of water in an open pit.
When the things of saṃsāra are encountered and experienced,
It is true that no wonderful essence is found.

573. Still, the number of men and women is the same.
It is easy for them to find each other.
If they desire each other, lust is a greater sin than copulation.
Thus, it is indeed right to seek the enjoyment of sex.

574. If we get used to something long enough,
There is nothing in this life that does not make us sad.
True divine dharma is the solace for this sadness.
At least once, it is certain to enter one's mind.

575. The fool who defends his ordinary perceptions
And the sage who conjures his constructed thoughts
Part ways at the crossroad and follow different paths.
They meet again on the edge of the three paths.[5]

576. Now, seeing the depths of the ocean of saṃsāra, [71]
If you are disenchanted and cannot bear it,

5. "The three paths" (*lam gsum*) refers to the Ganges River, which flows in three places: first, from Śiva's locks, second, into the human world, and third, into the underworld. "Meeting on the edge of the Ganges" is an allusion to meeting death on the banks of the Ganges, where traditionally many Indians have chosen to be cremated and their ashes thrown into the river.

I ask you to clad your body in saffron [robes]
And strive one-pointedly in the pacifying dharma.

577. In the auspicious ages of the past,
Tibetan scholars came to this noble land of India.
Endowed with the three trainings, they restrained the three doors.
Their ears would find such talk [of sex] unbearable.

578. As for me, I have little shame and great faith in women.
I am the kind who chooses the bad and discards the good.
Although I have not had the vows in my head for some time,
The guts of pretense were destroyed only recently.

579. The skills of fish are impressive in the water.
One is most familiar with what one has experienced.
With this in mind, it was my lot
To write this treatise with great effort.

580. If monks condemn it, that's not untoward.
If tāntrikas praise it, that's not unfitting.
To old Lugyal Bum, its benefit is small.
To young Sonam Thar,[6] its benefit is great.

581. The author is Gendun Chopel.
The place of composition is the city of Mathurā.
The difficult parts of the text were explained by an old brahmin.
The practical lessons were given by a Muslim girl.

6. Lugyal Bum and Sonam Thar are common male names in Gendun Chopel's home region of Amdo.

582. The explanation is rooted in the Indian treatises.
The verses are arranged in Tibetan style, easy to understand.
Thus, from the convergence of causes complete,
I feel that a marvelous fruit is certain to appear.

583. The monk Mi pham wrote from reading.
The wanton Chopel wrote from experience.
The difference in their power to grant blessings,
A passionate man and woman will know through practice.

584. Yet if there are faults of excess or deficiency here,
Being too much for those without desire,
Being too little for the passionate,
I apologize from my heart, concealing and hiding nothing. [72]

585. Do not blame a lowly person [like me],
Whatever faults might befall you:
A monastic friend undoing his way of life,
A narrow-minded poser losing his facade.

586. Through this virtue [of writing], may all like-minded friends
Cross the dark road of misty desires
And see the sky of the true nature of reality
From the summit of the sixteen peaks of pleasure.

587. Yudön, Gangā, Asali, and the others,
The women who joined with my body,
May they persist on the path, from bliss to bliss,
To arrive at great bliss, the place of *dharmakāya*.

588. May all humble people who live on this broad earth
Be delivered from the pit of merciless laws

And be able to indulge, with freedom,
In common enjoyments, so needed and right.

This *Kāmaśāstra* by Gendun Chopel—who traveled across the ocean of our own and others' sciences, eliminating misconceptions about the passion of desire through hearing, thinking, and experience—was completed in the latter part of the middle month of winter in the Tiger Year [January 1939] in the great city of Mathurā in Magadha near the banks of the glorious Yamuna River, while the radiance of a summer dawn was descending in the house of Gaṅgādeva from Pañcāla, a companion in the same practice. May there be virtue and goodness. Sarvamaṅgalam.

AFTERWORD: BACKGROUND TO *A TREATISE ON PASSION*

THE LIFE OF GENDUN CHOPEL

Gendun Chopel was born in 1903 in a village in the Repgong district of Amdo—at the time, the far northeastern area of Tibet, but today, part of China's Qinghai Province. His father was a respected lama of the Nyingma or "Ancient" sect of Tibetan Buddhism, which traces its roots to the visit to Tibet by the mysterious tantric yogin Padmasambhava in the late eighth century. Padmasambhava is said to have hidden many texts in the mountains, lakes, and valleys of Tibet in order that they might be discovered in the future, when the Tibetans were ready to receive them. These texts, called "treasures" (*gter ma*), would become some of the central works of the vast Nyingma canon. Gendun Chopel's father was an accomplished scholar of a section of the treasure literature called the "Heart Essence of the Great Expanse" (*Klong chen snying thig*).

At the age of five, Gendun Chopel was identified as an incarnate lama (*sprul sku*) of the Nyingma sect but was never formally invested in the position. Learning to read at a young age he memorized many prayers and was known as a precocious poet. His father, who had been his principal teacher, died when Gendun Chopel was a young boy; he continued his education at the traditional site of learning in Tibet, the Buddhist monastery. Around the age of twelve, he was ordained as a novice monk and entered the local Geluk monastery, before moving around 1920 to the great regional monastery of Labrang, one of the six great Geluk monasteries of Tibet, with some four thousand monks. Here, he quickly gained notoriety as a skilled debater. He was eventually invited to leave the monastery under uncertain circumstances; in a bitter poem, he wrote that monks who broke their vows and engaged in all manner of unseemly deeds were allowed to stay while good monks, like him, who kept their vows and devoted their lives to study, were expelled.[1]

In 1928, he left his mother, his sister, and his beloved Amdo, never to return. Accompanied by an uncle and a cousin, he set off on the four-month trek to the capital of Tibet, Lhasa, where he enrolled at Drepung, the largest monastery in the world, with over ten thousand monks. Unless monks were supported by their families, they had to earn money to pay for their food. Gendun Chopel worked as an artist, eventually receiving commissions for his paintings from aristocrats in the capital. By 1934, he had successfully completed the extensive scholastic curriculum of the Geluk academy but had not taken the examinations for the *geshe* degree. At that time, the Indian scholar and patriot Rahul Sankrityayan (1893–1963) arrived in Lhasa in search of Sanskrit manuscripts in the monasteries of southern Tibet. He required a guide, both to take him to the various sites and to negotiate with the abbots to allow a foreigner to examine the contents of their libraries. Gendun Chopel's teacher at Drepung recommended him for the job, and he accepted. At the conclusion of their expedition, Pandit Rahul, as he was called, invited Gendun Chopel to return with him to India.[2] As he wrote, "So on the eighteenth day of the winter month of *ra ba* of my thirty-second year [1934], I drank the water of the Ganges. During the entire winter of that year I stayed in Pāṭaliputra (Patna), with a sense of sadness, like that of an insect who has fallen into the middle of a lake."[3] He would not return to Tibet until 1945.

There was a long tradition of Sanskrit learning in Tibet; Gendun Chopel had himself studied it during his youth. However, after learning Sanskrit in India, he would come to mock the way that Sanskrit was taught in Tibet and the Sanskrit compositions of Tibetan scholars. During their travels in Tibet, it appears that Rahul Sankrityayan gave Gendun Chopel lessons in Sanskrit; he continued his studies after he reached India. During his years in India, Gendun Chopel read widely in the Sanskrit classics. He would translate selections from the Sanskrit play *Śakuntalā* and several chapters of both the *Rāmāyaṇa* and the *Bhagavad Gītā* from Sanskrit into Tibetan, and the *Dhammapada* from Pāli into Tibetan. He also is said to have retranslated Daṇḍin's seventh-century handbook on Sanskrit poetics, the *Mirror of Poetry* (*Kāvyādarśa*) from Sanskrit into Tibetan; he had studied the work in Tibetan during his youth. Indeed, in the records and accounts of his friends and students we find references to dozens of works—both translations and independent pieces—that he composed during his years in India; only a handful seem to have survived.[4]

Gendun Chopel's travels in India and Sri Lanka have been documented elsewhere; they need not be described in detail here.[5] He spent the final period of his time abroad, in 1944 and 1945, in West Bengal and Sikkim, where he became involved in discussions with a small group of Tibetans who would become the ill-fated Tibet Improvement Party, which sought democratic reforms in Tibet. He returned to Tibet in the summer of 1945.[6] He soon gathered a small circle of students, including both monks and aristocrats, to whom he taught the many things he had learned during his South Asian sojourn.[7] A year after his return to Tibet, in July 1946, the Tibetan government (at that time ruled by a regent while the Fourteenth Dalai Lama was in his minority) placed him under arrest, charging him with distributing counterfeit currency.[8] He maintained his innocence throughout his interrogation, which included flogging. Despite the pleas of his friends and supporters, he was incarcerated, eventually held in the prison at the foot of the Potala Palace, winter residence of the Dalai Lama.

He was released in 1950, the year of the Chinese invasion of Tibet. By most accounts, he emerged from prison a broken man, addicted to alcohol and opium. His extensive notes and writings from his time abroad had been confiscated, and he showed no interest in reviving his many projects. However, he dictated to a disciple his thoughts on Madhyamaka philosophy. This would be published posthumously as his controversial *Adornment for Nāgārjuna's Thought* (*Klu sgrub dgongs rgyan*).[9] In the fall of 1951, he became seriously ill, with symptoms consistent with cirrhosis of the liver. On September 9, he had to be helped to his roof to witness troops of the People's Liberation Army marching through the streets of Lhasa. He died in October, at the age of forty-eight. Late in his life, he is said to have summarized his life in four lines of verse:

A virtuous family, the lineage of monks, the way of a layman,
A time of abundance, a time of poverty,
The best of monks, the worst of laymen,
My body has changed so much in one lifetime.[10]

Our interest in this volume is not the end of Gendun Chopel's life, or his major prose works: *Grains of Gold*, *Guide for Traveling to the Sacred Sites of India*, the *White Annals*, or *Adornment for Nāgārjuna's Thought*. It is instead his longest work of poetry and the earliest extant complete work from his time in India. It is also his most famous work: *A Treatise on Passion* (*'Dod pa'i bstan bcos*). According to the colophon, it was completed "in the latter part of the middle month of winter in the Tiger Year in the great city of Mathurā in Magadha near the banks of the glorious Yamuna River." The Tiger Year of the Tibetan lunar calendar was 1938. He thus completed this work in early 1939, four years after his arrival in India.

In many ways Gendun Chopel's *Treatise on Passion* mirrors the complexities and contradictions that characterized the life of this most famous of modern Tibetan authors. Like its author, the work craves respect and recognition from Tibetan aristocrats and intellectuals, yet it mocks their sensibilities. The text celebrates the Indic sources of classical Tibetan culture, yet condemns contemporary Indian sexual mores. The text extols the ideals of a monastic life, yet questions the vow of celibacy that is its foundation. It demands the right to sexual freedom for the masses, yet is written for the educated few who could read literary Tibetan. Indeed, like its author, *A Treatise on Passion* remains something of an enigma within Gendun Chopel's oeuvre. The apparently simple question "Why did he write this text?" does not have a simple answer. One must first consider the larger question of the place of sexuality in the Buddhist tradition that Gendun Chopel knew so well.

BUDDHIST SEXUALITY

Throughout *A Treatise on Passion*, Gendun Chopel expresses his skepticism, often bordering on contempt, for the rules set forth by Buddhist monks to restrict sexual pleasure, both their own and that of others. If, as he claims, the *Treatise* is also a record of his own experiences, he violated a great many of those rules. In order to understand his text it is therefore important to have a general understanding of Buddhist views of human sexuality. It is a vast topic, and our presentation here must be brief.

We might begin with a well-known Buddhist creation myth. According to Buddhist doctrine, the cycle of birth and death has no beginning; there is no first cause, no unmoved mover. Yet various worlds are created and destroyed not by God but by the karma of sentient beings. First, a physical world forms, after which it begins to be populated. The first beings to be reborn in the world are humans, reborn from one of the heavens. At first, they are unlike the humans that they will become. They are luminous, they can fly, they have no need for food, and they have no gender. A frothy substance covers the surface of the earth. Eventually one of the beings tastes it. It is sweet. Others begin to consume it, causing their bodies to gain weight and density. Soon, they can no longer fly and their bodies lose their luster; the sun and the moon appear to light the sky. As they consume more of the frothy substance—which evolves into a kind of naturally growing rice—their bodies need to excrete waste, causing the lower orifices to develop; two sexes appear. Soon, one male and one female discover copulation. The other beings of the world are so disgusted by their copulation that they begin to throw clods of earth at them. In order to hide themselves from the eyes of others, the couple builds the first shelter.[11]

We see here a scene quite different from the Garden of Eden. The beings are not created by God, but by their own past deeds. In the beginning, they have no gender. Gender, sexuality, shelter, private property, society, and eventually government are all the result of a different kind of Fall than that described in Genesis. They are the consequences of the curiosity, and eventual greed, of beings who sought sensual pleasure; in this case, the pleasure of the sense of taste. Sexual pleasure is not something granted by

God; its origin can be traced back to a negative deed, the craving of the first inhabitants of this world. In the beginning, there was no gender. And the sex act itself is considered disgusting, so disgusting that it must take place in hiding.

According to Buddhist doctrine, all pleasure and pain is the result of deeds done in the past, with virtuous deeds resulting in feelings of mental and physical pleasure and nonvirtuous deeds resulting in feelings of mental and physical pain. Sexual pleasure is therefore regarded as a result of past virtues. Yet it is also presented as one of the obsessions of the Realm of Desire (*kāmadhātu*) in the Buddhist cosmos, so called because the beings born there are obsessed with the pleasures derived from the five senses of sight, hearing, taste, smell, and touch. Among the six realms of rebirth, the gods of the Realm of Desire are said to experience sexual bliss greater than that known by humans.

Indeed, sexual pleasure exists in all six heavens of the Realm of Desire, but in different ways, illustrating the ways in which, according to classical Buddhist doctrine (tantric Buddhism will be considered below), higher states are marked by more subtle pleasures and by less physical embodiment. Thus, in the two lowest heavens of the Realm of Desire—both of which, notably, are located on the surface of the earth, that is, the upper slopes and summit of Mount Meru, the central mountain of the Buddhist universe—sexual pleasure is derived from copulation. As one proceeds through the next four heavens, all located in the sky above Mount Meru, sexual pleasure is derived from more and more subtle, and less physical, means. Thus, as one advances through the four heavenly heavens, sexual pleasure is derived from embracing, holding hands, smiling at each other, and gazing at each other—orgasm by eye contact. As we shall discuss below, this hierarchy is reversed in presentations of tantric practice.

The strange dilemma of the Buddhist system is that, while sexual pleasure is not condemned, sexual desire is. Motivating the deeds that fructify as the myriad sufferings of the world are the so-called three poisons of desire, hatred, and ignorance, with *rāga*, the Sanskrit term rendered as "desire," having the sense of "passion," "excitement," and "becoming red." It thus connotes lust for an object of pleasure. Deeds motivated by such desire both produce experiences of pain in the future and increase attachment to the world, thus perpetuating the powerless wandering through the six realms of *saṃsāra*.

This leads to an ironic element of Buddhist ascetic theory. When the Buddha seeks to dissuade his half brother, the newly ordained Nanda, from returning to his bride, he takes him to Indra's heaven, where the sexual partners of the gods—celestial nymphs called *apsaras*—are far more beautiful than Nanda's wife. They are so beautiful, in fact, that it is only through the Buddha's protection that Nanda does not die from simply seeing them. The gods making love to these women were in their previous lives ascetics who practiced celibacy. As Aśvaghoṣa describes them, "Eternally youthful and occupied solely with lovemaking, they were a communal enjoyment for heaven-dwellers who had earned merit. Taking these heavenly women as lovers was no fault, just an acceptance of the rewards of asceticism."[12] Thus, the karmic result of abstaining from sexual pleasure in this life is greater sexual pleasure in the next life. Yet, like all pleasures in *saṃsāra*, the lifetimes of the gods also end. All desire must be extinguished in order for one to be liberated from the cycle of birth and death.

Other human needs—for sustenance and shelter, for example—may be pursued without negative effect as long as they are pursued without an attitude of strong attachment to them. Thus, Buddhist texts do not find fault with great wealth, as long as one is willing to give it away. We recall that in his last lifetime before his birth as Prince Siddhārtha, the future Buddha was born as Prince Vessantara, who gave away all that was dear to him, including his children and his wife. Yet sexual pleasure cannot take place without desire and sexual pleasure cannot be given to another without arousing attachment (except for certain advanced beings, as described below). Sexual passion is required for progeny, and Buddhist texts extol the importance of the happy family, at least for the laity; the term sometimes translated as "layman" is *gṛhastha* or "householder," a father of a family. Sexual pleasure cannot therefore be forbidden to such a man (and discussions of sexuality for the laity in Buddhism are overwhelmingly from the male perspective), but it can be regulated.

Rules of the Laity

Buddhist ethics are typically set forth in terms of ten negative deeds that are to be avoided. There are three committed with the body: killing, stealing, and sexual misconduct; four committed with speech: lying, divisive speech, harsh speech, and senseless speech; and three committed with the mind: covetousness, harmful intent, and wrong view.

The term "sexual misconduct" is *kāmamithyācāra* in Sanskrit—literally, "improper passionate conduct." For Gendun Chopel, the main explication of what constitutes sexual misconduct would have been Tsong kha pa's *Great Treatise on the Stages of the Path to Enlightenment* (*Lam rim chen mo*). There we read that four elements constitute sexual misconduct: an inappropriate person, an improper body part, an improper place, or an improper time. Described from the perspective of the male, the women with whom one should not have sexual intercourse include one's mother, the wives of others, nuns, unmarried women under the protection of their families, and women protected by the king. Intercourse with men and eunuchs is also prohibited. Sex with a prostitute for whom one has paid is permitted. Improper body parts essentially include anything other than the vagina. Thus, oral sex and anal sex are prohibited, as is intercrural sex and manual masturbation.[13] Improper places include where the dharma is taught, a *stūpa*, and the vicinity of a religious teacher or one's parents. Improper times are during menstruation, during pregnancy, or when a mother is nursing, is ill, or has taken a one-day vow of celibacy. According to another source, sexual intercourse during the day is also improper. During those times when intercourse is permitted, doing so more than five times a night is improper.[14]

The karmic consequences of deeds of sexual misconduct generally entail rebirth as a ghost or in one of the hells. Indeed, in Buddhist representations of the various hells, the tortures suffered by those who engaged in deviant sex acts are vividly portrayed.[15] According to Buddhist karmic theory, in addition to the "fruitional effect" (*vipākaphala*) of an action that produces the next lifetime, there are residual effects, called "causally concordant effects" (*niṣyandaphala*) that occur in subsequent lifetimes. Thus, a person who has committed murder and has been reborn in hell may have a short lifespan the next time he is reborn as a human. In the case of sexual misconduct, such causally concordant effects include being reborn as a woman who is raped, being reborn as a hermaphrodite, eunuch, or impotent male, and being married to an unfaithful wife. In addition, there is something called the "dominant effect" (*adhipatiphala*), sometimes translated as the "environmental effect," which determines the environment of the rebirth following that in which the main effect is suffered. In the case of sexual misconduct, one is reborn in a place that is dirty and foul smelling.

The Monastic Code

Before turning to the monastic code, it is useful to briefly consider the sex life of the most famous of Buddhist monks, the Buddha himself. According to the well-known story, he was born as Prince Siddhārtha and spent the first twenty-nine years of his life in the palace, shielded from knowledge of the world and its sufferings. The various accounts of his days as a prince make it clear that he was strong and virile, skilled in all of the manly arts, including, according to a list in the *Extensive Play* (*Lalitavistara*), "the signs of women" (*strīlakṣaṇa*) and methods of copulation (*vaiśika*).[16] His palace is populated by beautiful women who provide him with pleasure. His virility and virtue allow him to win the hand of a beautiful maiden named Yaśodharā (in some accounts he has three wives). It is only after his marriage and (according to most accounts) after the birth of his son Rāhula that he decides to leave the palace to seek a state beyond suffering.

In the *Deeds of the Buddha* (*Buddhacarita*) by Aśvaghoṣa, a work usually dated to the second century CE, there is a telling scene in which his charioteer takes Prince Siddhārtha to a park, where beautiful women await him. Having already learned of aging, sickness, and death, he rebuffs their advances. When his friend asks him why he does not make love to the women, the prince replies:

I show no contempt for pleasures of sense,
  I know that people are obsessed with them;
But knowing that the world is transient,
  my heart finds no delight in them at all.
For if old age, sickness, and death,
  these three things were not to exist,
I would also have found delight
  in delightful pleasures of the senses. (6.85–86)[17]

It is noteworthy that, at least in this account, the prince shows no particular disdain for women or even for sensual pleasures. Yet in a world marked by aging, sickness, and death, they hold no allure. He would thus soon leave the world, and six years hence achieve enlightenment under the Bodhi tree, attracting a group of disciples.

During the first years of the Buddha's community, the monks were not required to take vows. His first disciples all gained one of the four stages of enlightenment (stream enterer, once returner, never returner, and *arhat*) shortly after meeting the Buddha, sometimes after simply hearing a discourse. The conduct of someone who has achieved one of these four stages is said to be naturally ethical and thus rules to regulate their conduct were unnecessary. However, as the fame of the Buddha grew, he began to attract disciples whose progress on the path was less rapid and whose motivations for becoming a monk were less noble. As a result, there arose the need for rules to regulate this growing community. According to various traditions, this need first occurred five, twelve, or twenty years after the Buddha's enlightenment. Whenever it occurred, however, the Buddha did not set forth a comprehensive code of conduct. Instead, the monastic code grew more organically. It was only after a particular transgression occurred that the Buddha would establish a rule against it. Because the initial misdeed was not a transgression at the time that it was committed, the original transgressor would not incur punishment. Each rule in what would become a large and complex monastic code (with 253 vows to abstain from specific transgressions in the Mūlasarvāstivāda vinaya, for example) would therefore have its own narrative of how it came to be established, with much of the vinaya literature devoted to such narratives. As one might expect, the first vow that the Buddha had to establish was the vow requiring celibacy. The story of what led to its establishment is quite telling.

A young man named Sudinna was the heir to his family's fortune. After hearing the Buddha teach, he asked him for permission to join the order of monks. Although Sudinna was married (but still childless), the Buddha told him that he must receive the permission of his parents. He was their only child, and they initially refused, eventually relenting when he lay on the ground and refused to eat. After his ordination, Sudinna left his home and went to Vajji. However, the region soon suffered a famine, and monks were unable to gather alms for their sustenance. Sudinna, knowing that his home region continued to prosper, returned there. Recognized by some of his relatives, he was able to gather sufficient food for himself and his fellow monks. When his parents learned of his return, they invited him home for a meal, placing great piles of gold in the room and instructing his wife to dress in all of her finery. They implored Sudinna to accept the gold and return to lay life, explaining that it was possible to both lead the life of a layman and to perform meritorious deeds. However, he told them to place the gold in bags and throw it in the river because the gold would only bring them fear. When his wife asked Sudinna whether he had abandoned her so that he could consort with celestial nymphs, he responded indignantly, addressing his wife as "sister." She fainted at the word.

His mother then explained to him that if his parents died without an heir, all of the wealth and property they had accumulated would be forfeited to the state. If he would not return to the family, she asked Sudinna if he would at least father a son. He agreed. As arranged by his mother, he met his wife in the forest when she was fertile, took off his monk's robes, and had intercourse with her (three times). She conceived and bore a son who, according to the story, also became a monk. Sudinna never returned to his wife nor apparently felt any desire to do so.

Sudinna had broken no rule or vow, but he was overcome with remorse and guilt. When his fellow monks expressed concern about his wretched demeanor, he told them what he had done. They in turn informed the Buddha.[18] The Buddha's response was sufficiently harsh that King Milinda later wondered whether it disproved the claim that the Buddha was always courteous in his speech.[19] It was a legitimate question, since the Buddha said:

> Worthless man, haven't I taught the Dhamma in many ways for the fading of passion, the sobering of intoxication, the subduing of thirst, the destruction of attachment, the severing of the round, the ending of craving, dispassion, cessation, unbinding? Haven't I in many ways advocated abandoning sensual pleasures, comprehending sensual perceptions, subduing sensual thirst, destroying sensual thoughts, calming sensual fevers?
>
> Worthless man, it would be better that your penis be stuck into the mouth of a poisonous snake than into a woman's vagina. It would be better that your penis be stuck into the mouth of a black viper than into a woman's vagina. It would be better that your penis be stuck into a pit of burning embers, blazing and glowing, than into a woman's vagina. Why is that? For that reason you would undergo death or death-like suffering, but you would not on that account, at the break-up of the body, after death, fall into deprivation, the bad destination, the abyss, hell.[20]

The Buddha's vivid castigation of Sudinna contrasts the intense but short-term suffering that would result from placing his penis in the mouth of a viper to the centuries of suffering in hell that result from placing his penis in the vagina of a woman. The implication is not that sexual intercourse itself leads to hell but that everything that follows from sexual intercourse—wife, family, property—entail an entrapment in a world fraught with worldly concerns that in turn foment the greed and the malice that motivate deeds that result in rebirth in the infernal realms. In the Buddha's metaphor, the penis becomes trapped in the vagina, that is, the entanglements created by sexual intercourse (which in this case means heterosexual intercourse) lead only to suffering. The Buddha's warning to all monks of the dangers of physical intimacy with a woman seems, then, to have little to do with love. Instead, for the penis to enter the vagina is for the monk to reenter the world that he has renounced and to remain trapped there.

Because there had been no formal prohibition of sexual intercourse prior to Sudinna's filial deed, he was not expelled from the order. However, from that point on, sexual intercourse (defined as the penetration of an orifice even to the depth of a sesame seed) would be the first of four transgressions that entail expulsion from the community of monks. The other three were the killing of a human, stealing, and lying about one's spiritual attainments.

Although the Buddha condemns craving and calls for the calming of "sensual fevers," the story of the monastic rule of celibacy is not so much about love, or lust, but about familial obligation, and about property. Sudinna's wife does not go in search of her husband out of love for him; she is taken to him by her mother-in-law. Sudinna does seek sexual pleasure with his wife but has intercourse with her in order to produce an heir for his family. It is important to note that love and lust are not absent from the story because of some cultural reticence to represent them. Stories of love and longing abound in classical Indian literature, including Buddhist literature. Sudinna makes love to his wife because he is a dutiful son. Yet the Buddha condemns the deed.

It is not that the Buddha somehow imagined that if the world were celibate, suffering would come to an end. Human birth is something that is praised again and again in Buddhist literature, but only as the rare moment of the opportunity to escape from birth. In the early tradition, the goal of the Buddhist path is not creation but extinction, like a flame going out. Even the Buddha's family line came to an end when Rāhula, the sole son and heir of the Buddha, also became a celibate monk. Thus, whenever a monk is ordained, he receives this instruction:

> The Blessed One has in many ways condemned sexual pleasure and attachment to sexual pleasure and longing for sexual pleasure and obsession with sexual pleasure. He has praised giving up sexual pleasure, has commended, revered, praised and extolled its abandonment, removal, dissipation, the separation from passion, its uprooting, abatement and decline. Since, Venerable, from this day forward, you must avert your eyes in regard to a woman with lascivious thoughts and not even look at her, how much more must you not couple and engage in unchaste intercourse! Venerable, the knowing and seeing Blessed One, the Tathāgata, arhat, completely and perfectly Awakened One has said: "If a monk who is in conformity with the rules of training together with the other monks engages in unchastity and intercourse without having given back the rules of training, removed the rules of training—even if it is with an animal—that monk, because he is defeated, is one denied the right of living with a community." If a monk has done such a thing, immediately upon doing so he is not a monk, not an ascetic, not a son of the Buddha, and has perished from the state of a monk. For him the character of an ascetic is destroyed, perished, disrupted, fallen, defeated, and for him the character of an ascetic cannot be restored—like a palmyra tree with its top lopped off is incapable of becoming green again, incapable of again sprouting growth or gaining fullness. You, from this day forward, must make effort to carefully guard your thought by remembering and attending to what is not to be practiced, and not to be done, and to the abstention from what is not to be practiced.[21]

The story of Sudinna, and the subsequent formulation of the vow, suggests that the Buddha does not simply censure sex because of the passions that produce it. He also censures sex for what sex leads to: birth and rebirth, the institutions that sustain them, and, above all, the wide range of destructive thoughts and emotions they produce. These are the engines of *saṃsāra*, the cycle of birth and death, the cycle from which the Buddha sought, and found, liberation. To engage in sexual intercourse is to engage in the world; a person who does so cannot be counted as a monk, an ascetic, and a son of the Buddha.

The Buddha would also establish an order of nuns, but only when he was urged to do so by his stepmother, and only after predicting that his agreement to do so would shorten the duration of his teachings in the world. The denigration of women and graphic descriptions of the foulness of the female body would become standard elements of Buddhist texts composed over the long history of Buddhism in India, making their way across Asia.[22]

The Mahāyāna

The Mahāyāna has sometimes been portrayed as largely a lay movement, opening the path to enlightenment to all, with an ethos that was somehow more "liberal" than the conservative and hidebound "Hīnayāna." Such a portrayal is problematic from a number of perspectives. First, scholars have yet to identify the origins of the Mahāyāna with any historical or doctrinal precision. Indeed, it is difficult to say with any confidence that the Mahāyāna was a single and self-conscious movement in India, rather than a retrospective designation, primarily of a large corpus of predominantly autonomous texts referred to as the "Mahāyāna sūtras," whose composition seemed to begin some four centuries after the passing of the Buddha. Despite the presence of lay bodhisattvas in some Mahāyāna sūtras, most famously the *Teaching of Vimalakīrti* (*Vimalakīrtinirdeśa*), it appears from what is known about the authors of the Mahāyāna treatises (*śāstra*) and from the reports of Chinese pilgrims that the leading figures of what is referred to as the Mahāyāna were monks. Some but not all Mahāyāna sūtras, most famously the *Lotus Sūtra*, did proclaim the path to buddhahood as open to all, yet it also condemned to hell those who failed to affirm that the *Lotus Sūtra* was spoken by the Buddha. The term Hīnayāna, "vile vehicle" or "base vehicle" (often translated euphemistically as "lesser vehicle"), is a term of abuse that appears in Mahāyāna works to refer to those who regard the Mahāyāna sūtras as spurious. Scholars tend to refer to the Buddhist traditions that preceded "the Mahāyāna" with the term "mainstream Buddhism," suggesting both its foundational nature as well as the possibility that the Mahāyāna remained a minority movement throughout its long history in India.

The implications of all this for Buddhist views of sexuality are important; on questions of monastic celibacy and of the sexual mores of the Buddhist laity, no revolutionary changes occurred in the Mahāyāna. Indeed, in a famous Mahāyāna sūtra, the *Questions of Ugra* (*Ugraparipṛcchā*), the married lay bodhisattva is enjoined to practice celibacy at all times: "Moreover, O Eminent Householder, the householder bodhisattva who lives in the home is pure in his practice of celibacy. He does not act on desires even in his mind; how much less so does he actually participate in sexual intercourse or enter into erotic love?"[23] Elsewhere in the same text, a litany of similes (in sets of three) is provided to aid the householder bodhisattva in developing aversion for his wife. He is to think of her, for example, as a demon, an ogre, and a hag; as sickness, old age, and death; as a huge wolf, a huge sea monster, and a huge cat; a black snake, a crocodile, and a demon that causes epilepsy; and as swollen, shriveled, and diseased.[24] In the apocryphal *Brahmā's Net Sūtra* (*Fanwang jing*), the central source for the bodhisattva vows in East Asian Buddhism, we read, "A son of the Buddha must refrain from sexual misconduct, by committing an improper act himself, by causing someone else to engage in such acts, or by indulging in sexual relations with women."[25]

Two changes, however, in the domain of sexuality are to be found in the Mahāyāna. In the Mahāyāna sūtras a host of bodhisattvas are introduced into the Buddhist pantheon, endowed with all manner of magical powers. Some of these extend into sexuality. Thus, a bodhisattva named Priyaṃkara ("Causing Pleasure") was so handsome that a woman died of lust but was reborn as a male deity in the Heaven of the Thirty-Three.[26] There are other stories of bodhisattvas using sexual intercourse to "tame" women, that is, to bring them to the dharma, including the Buddha himself, who, as an ascetic in a previous lifetime, had practiced celibacy for forty-two thousand years. Yet he gave up his vow of celibacy for twelve years in order to live with a woman who would have otherwise died without his love.[27]

In terms of doctrine, perhaps the most consequential change that occurs in Mahāyāna literature has to do with the bodhisattva vows. The bodhisattva vow is generally represented as the bodhisattva's promise to liberate all beings from suffering. However, in Buddhist India (and hence in Tibet) the bodhisattva vow also refers to a specific set of vows that the bodhisattva promises not to transgress, such as the promise not to praise oneself and belittle others, not to refuse to accept an apology, and not to deny that the Mahāyāna sūtras are the word of the Buddha.[28] Among the secondary infractions of the bodhisattva vows is the failure to commit any of the physical or verbal nonvirtuous deeds in order to benefit another. As noted above, in Buddhist ethical theory, ten nonvirtuous deeds are enumerated as the chief causes of suffering in saṃsāra. The first three are physical: killing, stealing, and sexual misconduct. The next four are verbal: lying, divisive speech, harsh speech, and senseless speech. The last three are mental: covetousness, harmful intent, and wrong view. Hence, the bodhisattva vows to be willing to kill, steal, engage in sexual misconduct, lie, speak divisively, speak harshly, and speak senselessly if it will benefit others. Sexual intercourse, with the right motivation, would seem to be permitted. However, the commentaries specify that this is allowed only for lay bodhisattvas, not for bodhisattvas who are monks. This would confirm the characterization of the Mahāyāna as maintaining the ordained monk as its paradigmatic practitioner.

Buddhist Tantra

In the long accepted narrative of the history of Buddhism, it is with the rise of tantra that Buddhist attitudes toward sexuality are transformed, for good or for ill, depending on one's perspective. One need only read the opening lines of the *Guhyasamāja*, perhaps the most famous of all Buddhist tantras: "Thus did I hear. At one time the Bhagavan was residing in the vaginas of the women who are the *vajra* essence of the body, speech, and mind of all the tathāgathas." And, indeed, references to intercourse with a tantric "consort," often an adolescent low-caste girl, abound in Buddhist tantric literature. Yet it remains unclear how many of such references were regarded as injunctions to be followed, how many of the reversals that appear so often in tantric literature—of caste hierarchies, of dietary rules, of sexual mores—were rhetorical rather than practical. By the time Buddhist tantra came to Tibet, there was much scholastic agonizing over whether the consort was to be real or imagined, over whether the ordained monk could engage in sexual yoga, and, if so, what advanced stage of the path must he have achieved in order to do so. An entire genre of literature, called the "three vows" (*sdom gsum*) evolved to ponder the question of the compatibility of the monk's vows, the bodhisattva vows, and the tantric vows.[29] Was it possible to take and maintain all three? We thus find in Tibetan Buddhism a particular dilemma. Sexual intercourse is prohibited in the vinaya, the code of discipline that was seen as the foundation of the monastic community. Yet, as we will see below, in order to achieve buddhahood, the avowed goal of all Tibetan Buddhist practitioners, one must engage in sexual intercourse. This contradiction between prohibition and promotion is one that Gendun Chopel would exploit in his treatise.

Who engaged in tantric sex, whether in India or Tibet, is a huge question, and one that is not easy to answer.[30] For the purposes of this volume, the more important question is: What was the doctrinal foundation for the practice of sexual yoga in Tibetan Buddhism?

Tsong kha pa (1357–1419)—regarded as the founder of the Geluk sect where Gendun Chopel was a monk—wrote extensively on the use of sexual yoga in a number of works.[31] Underlying his argument was a particular tantric view of human physiology. According to this tantric physiology, winds (*prāṇa*) or subtle energies course through the body in a network of seventy-two thousand channels (*nāḍi*). These winds serve as the vehicles for consciousness. Among all these channels, the most important is the central channel (*avadhūtī*), which runs from the genitals upward to the crown of the head, then curves down (according to some systems) to end in the space between the eyes. Parallel to the central channel are the right and left channels, which wrap around it at several points, creating constrictions or knots that prevent wind from moving through the central channel. At these points of constriction, there are also networks of smaller channels that radiate throughout the body. These points are called wheels (*cakra*). These are often enumerated as seven: at the forehead, the crown of the head, the throat, the heart, the navel, the base of the spine, and the opening of the sexual organ.

Located inside the central channel at the heart *cakra* is what is called the indestructible drop. This drop, white on the top and red on the bottom, encases the subtlest wind and the subtlest form of consciousness, called the mind of clear light. According to Tsong kha pa, in order to achieve buddhahood, this subtlest form of consciousness must realize the subtlest nature of reality: emptiness (*śūnyatā*). However, in this system, the mind of clear light is locked within the indestructible drop and thus inaccessible. It is fully revealed only at the moment of death, when, as part of the process of rebirth, the indestructible drop opens, and the mind of clear light dawns in a vision said to be like the autumn sky at dawn, after the moon has set and the sun has not risen, with darkness dispelled. If it is not recognized, the mind of clear light goes on to the next lifetime and the process of rebirth is repeated. However, the mind of clear light is also manifest briefly at other moments in life, such as when one falls asleep or wakes up, when one enters into and rises from a dream, and, crucially, during orgasm. The doctrinal foundation for the practice of sexual yoga, therefore, is to gain access to the mind of clear light and to use it to achieve buddhahood.

This is not easily done, and it is said that only the most rare disciples are able to use the desire of sexual union as a means of achieving buddhahood. The *Saṃpuṭa Tantra* says: "Looking, smiling, holding hands, the two embracing make four; the four tantras abide in the manner of worms." Here, the allusion is to the four categories of tantra: action (*kriyā*), performance (*caryā*), yoga, and highest yoga (*niruttarayoga*), with highest yoga considered supreme. In the passage, the levels of subtlety of pleasure observed among the gods of the Buddhist heavens are reversed, with followers of action tantra only able to use the pleasure that arises from looking, followers of performance tantra only able to use the pleasure arising from smiling, and followers of yoga tantra only able to use the pleasure of holding hands. It is only the followers of Highest Yoga Tantra who can use the pleasure that arises from embracing (which here, unlike in the description of the heavens, refers to sexual union). The final line, "the four tantras abide in the manner of worms" refers to the particular homeopathy of Buddhist tantra, where, just as a thorn is used to extract a thorn and water is used to flush water from the ear, desire is used to destroy desire. In the ancient ecology of India, it was believed that the worms found when one broke open a rotten tree had been born from the wood and also consume the wood. Here the bliss that arises from desire is used to destroy desire and achieve buddhahood; it is called "making desire into the path" (*chags pa lam byed*). For example, the *Vajraḍākinī Tantra* says:

That which chains the foolish,
Is that which frees the wise.
Through this practice of sexual union
The wise consume the entire triple world.[32]

In Highest Yoga Tantra, regarded in the Geluk system as the supreme form of tantric practice—and the only form of practice that can bestow buddhahood—making desire into the path means sexual intercourse, first in visualization (with what is called the "wisdom consort") and later in the flesh (with what is called the "action consort"). The claim is that the achievement of buddhahood is impossible without sexual union and that all buddhas of the past, including Śākyamuni, have achieved buddhahood in this way. This view is succinctly captured in an oft-cited passage from the *Laghusaṃvara Tantra*: "As for Secret Mantra devoid of the seal of a consort, this cannot lead embodied beings to attainment."[33] Commenting on the *Cakrasaṃvara Tantra*, Tsong kha pa writes, "Seeing this crucial point, from the fifteenth up to the twenty-fourth chapter of the root tantra, only the topic of how to engage in union with qualified consorts has been presented. This subject is presented further in many other chapters as well."[34]

The clear light of death is experienced by all beings, but it is rarely noticed. This leaves the state of mind born of sexual bliss as the only viable opportunity for the yogin to utilize the subtle innate mind and fuse it with insight into emptiness, the ultimate truth. Thus, the Indian tantric master Saraha asks: "If those who sport in the bliss that dwells between the vajra and the lotus are unable to make use of it, how will they fulfill the hopes of the three worlds?"[35] That is, how will they achieve buddhahood?

There is a complex process in Highest Yoga Tantra of how sexual energy induces states of great bliss, with the yogin's mind becoming progressively free from all forms of ego consciousness as well as subject-object duality. Through manipulation of the energies flowing within the channels, bliss is induced. A key part of the technique is the "igniting" of the inner heat (*gtum mo*), located at the navel, which then causes the "drops" within the channels to melt downward, inducing progressively deeper levels of bliss. The inner heat comes to be ignited, setting the entire process in motion, through the stimulation of sexual energy, especially through sexual union. This is described, for example, in the *Vajramālā Tantra*:

The hero and the yoginī in union,
As the two secret tips touch each other
Through perfect conjoining of the organs,
They become victorious in space itself.
The wind created within the space,
By this the flame blazes forth.
Within the seventy-two thousand channels,
Elements are awakened, and this flame
Melts bodhicitta drops of great bliss,
The supreme state among all bliss.
Having melted, it abides in the channels,
Turning the three vajras [of body, speech, and mind] into a
single reality.[36]

This bliss, however, must also be manipulated. An additional element of tantric sexual practice is the so-called holding and spreading (*'dzin bkram*) techniques to prevent ejaculation, a technique that Gendun Chopel describes in verses 540–41. Certain Highest Yoga Tantras list progressive levels of bliss—joy, extraordinary joy, supreme joy, and innate joy—that occur as the essential drops melted through inner heat flow from the crown chakra to the throat, from the throat chakra to the heart, from the heart chakra to the navel, and finally from the navel chakra to the sexual organ. These are the "four joys of the sequential order." Techniques are set forth to bring about the "four joys of the reverse order," whereby the melted drops are drawn upward. These joys of reverse order lead to deeper and more refined levels of sexual bliss as the drop progresses upward through the central channel. In order for this to occur, the yogin must engage in techniques for "holding and spreading" the essential drops so that the "fault of emission" does not occur. In his *Five Stages of Completion in One Sitting*, for example, Tsong kha pa presents a well-known technique that involves pressing your two hands forcefully on your chest with your palms closed into fists, and glancing forcefully upward with a single-pointed focus on a syllable visualized at the crown of your head.[37]

That sexual yoga is essential to enlightenment is anticipated in the four initiations or empowerments (*abhiṣekha*) of Highest Yoga Tantra. The first, called the vase empowerment, is performed in public and entails a series of purifications. In the second, the secret empowerment, the disciple presents his master with a fully qualified consort. The consort, representing wisdom (*prajñā*), and the master, representing method (*upāya*), then engage in sexual union. A drop of the fluid that results from their union, called *bodhicitta*, is then placed on the tongue of the disciple, who swallows it. The third initiation is called "knowledge of the wisdom," with "wisdom" referring to the consort. The disciple then engages in sexual union, with the same consort from the second initiation, with their union resulting in increasing levels of bliss. This bliss causes a drop to ascend through the central channel. In the fourth empowerment, the yogin seeks to attain the state of innate bliss with the mind of clear light. In many renditions of the second, third, and fourth empowerment, sexual union occurs in visualization.

As in the general Mahāyāna path, the wisdom of emptiness remains the heart of the path to enlightenment, and the attainment of enlightenment involves dismantling all forms of objectification and conceptualization. What changes in the Vajrayāna is the notion that this insight into emptiness, the ultimate truth, must take place at the subtlest level of consciousness where the mind is free from all forms of dualism. This subtle level of consciousness can only be brought about through generating the experience of great bliss. The goal is a complete union of bliss and emptiness, a blissful mind fused with the knowledge of emptiness, the ultimate truth.

The doctrine that sexual yoga is essential to enlightenment immediately raises the question of whether such practices are permitted for monks, who have taken a vow of celibacy. This is one of the questions considered in the extensive "three vows" literature in Tibet, which considers how one maintains the *prātimokṣa*, bodhisattva, and tantric vows. On the question of the practice of sexual yoga by a monk, there is a range of opinion. Some point to Atiśa's famous declaration in his *Lamp for the Path to Enlightenment* (*Byang chub lam sgron*) that, "for those who know reality, there is no fault" (*de nyid rig la nyes pa med*)—that is, for a monk who has gained a profound understanding of emptiness, sexual yoga does not constitute an infraction of the vow of celibacy. Others, however, point to the story that Tsong kha pa, who had such an understanding, chose not to "rely on a consort" until after his death (while in the intermediate state) in order to demonstrate his commitment to celibacy.[38]

It is important to note that, despite some claims that tantric Buddhism raises the status of women, in the great majority of cases, the tantric consort is presented as an essential tool for the enlightenment of the male. Indeed, the common description of the ideal consort as a low-caste sixteen-year-old (or younger) girl is meant to suggest the miscegenation of caste mixing—the breaking of yet another taboo (such as using the unclean left hand) in order to use impurity to destroy impurity. At the same time, a number of Tibetan authors, including Tsong kha pa himself in a text that Gendun Chopel would have likely known, state unequivocally that women can also achieve buddhahood through the practice of sexual yoga.[39]

To recognize Gendun Chopel's allusions in his *Treatise on Passion*, it is therefore necessary to understand the different vision of enlightenment presented in the tantras, where bringing sexual bliss into the path becomes key. In incorporating the role of desire, especially of sexual desire, into the path, the Vajrayāna presents a radical transformation of how buddhahood is envisioned. Buddhahood is no longer characterized primarily in negative terms of a *dharmakāya* that is an absolute absence of all characterizations. Buddhahood is a state where the entire being—not just the mind, but the body, and the emotions—have all become perfected. Like turning base metals into gold, all aspects of the unenlightened, including the afflictions, are transformed into enlightened attributes.

AN OVERVIEW OF THE TEXT

A Treatise on Passion is an odd work, at least at first sight. It jumps from folk wisdom about how moles on the face predict a woman's future, to railings against the hypocrisy of monks and brahmins, to evocations of profound tantric states, to the sexual proclivities of women of various regions of India, to difficult (and difficult to translate) sexual positions, to moving paeans to erotic love. One reason for the diversity of topics is that Gendun Chopel had multiple motivations in composing the text. By examining them in turn, the contents of his *Treatise on Passion* come into sharper focus.

Indian Buddhists enumerated five traditional "sciences" (or literally, "foundations of knowledge," *vidyāsthāna*): grammar and composition (*śabda*), logic (*hetu*), medicine (*cikitsā*), crafts (*śilpakarman*), and the "inner knowledge" (*adhyātmavidyā*), that is, knowledge of the Buddhist scriptures. Although Tibetan Buddhism is sometimes represented as concerned exclusively with the last of these, in fact, all five of the Indian sciences were highly valued in Tibet; one was not considered fully educated without at least some knowledge of all five. The most renowned scholar in this regard was the great Sakya Paṇḍita (1182–1251), who brought the Sanskrit genre of *nītiśāstra* ("treatises on moral conduct") to Tibet with his famous collection of aphorisms called *Eloquent Sayings of Sakya* (*Sa skya legs bshad*). He also composed a treatise on music (*rol mo'i bstan bcos*). Sanskrit studies remained an important topic in all sects of Tibetan Buddhism, producing such luminaries as Tāranātha (1575–1634) among the Jo nang, Situ Panchen Chökyi Jungné (1700–1774) among the Kagyu, and Ju Mi pham (discussed below) among the Nyingma, along with many others.

Among Tibetan scholars of the twentieth century, perhaps none was more dedicated to the Sanskrit sciences than Gendun Chopel. As he writes in *Grains of Gold*, describing the Tibetan people, "Everything we do with our body, our speech, and our mind: the manner in which our scholars express their analysis, our style of composition, our clothing, our religious rituals, all of these are permeated by Indian influence as a sesame seed is permeated by its oil, so much so that when it is necessary to provide a metaphor in a poem, only the names of Indian rivers, mountains, and flowers are deemed suitable."[40]

Among his several projects during his years in South Asia was to bring some of the Sanskrit classics to a Tibetan audience. In *Grains of Gold,* he wrote at length about the great Sanskrit poets, and he devoted one of the longest chapters of the book to recounting stories from the *purāṇas* about Hindu deities, stories that were not known in Tibet. He translated sections of the *Bhagavad Gītā,* the *Rāmāyaṇa,* and *Śakuntalā* into Tibetan. He is also said to have made a new translation from Sanskrit into Tibetan of Daṇḍin's *Mirror of Poetry* (*Kāvyādarśa*), a work that he had studied in Tibetan translation in his youth. *A Treatise on Passion* must be understood as part of this project.

Works on erotica, or *kāmaśāstra* (literally, "treatises on passion," the very title of Gendun Chopel's text), form an important genre of Sanskrit belles lettres, with many works beyond the famous *Kāmasūtra* of Vātsyāyana. Yet, unlike other Sanskrit genres, only one work of Indian erotica had been translated into Tibetan, a text called *Kāmaśāstra,* only 255 lines long, by one Surūpa. It is found in the tantra (*rgyud*) section of the "translation of treatises" (*bstan 'gyur*) section of the Tibetan canon. Surūpa presents the types of women and men, cures for impotence, which body parts to bite on which days of the month, auspicious and inauspicious days for intercourse, and various sexual positions.[41]

The phrase "sixty-four arts of love" was known in Tibet, especially (and somewhat ironically) to monks of the Geluk sect, who would recite in the daily assembly the "Offering to the Lama" (*Bla ma mchod pa*), composed by Losang Chökyi Gyaltsen (1570–1662), the First Panchen Lama and teacher of the Fifth Dalai Lama. Among the long list of things offered (in visualization) to the teacher, one finds:

I even offer beautiful and magical consorts
With the glory of pleasing youth,
Skilled in the sixty-four arts of love,
A host of messengers field-born, mantra-born, and innate.[42]

One assumes that, despite the storied powers of memorization of Tibetan monks, few could enumerate the sixty-four arts of love. Furthermore, Tibet did not have an indigenous genre of erotic literature.

This is not to say that Tibetans did not enjoy stories about sex. There are, for example, stories about Aku Tönpa, a trickster figure who uses all manner of stratagems to have sex, especially with Buddhist nuns. However, these stories are more bawdy than erotic. In addition, there are a number of Tibetan tantric yogins, notably Drukpa Kunlek (1455–1529), who used explicitly sexual language, especially of copulation, as a metaphor for key elements of Vajrayāna practice and advanced meditative states. However, no one in the history of Tibetan literature had written a work as long, and as explicit, as Gendun Chopel's treatise. He sent a copy of the manuscript to the Tibetan aristocrat Kashöpa shortly after he completed it, and it circulated only in manuscript form during his lifetime. It is said to have created a sensation among the Lhasa aristocrats who read it, attracting some and repelling others. Gendun Chopel often portrayed himself as an ignored and misunderstood genius; he was likely delighted by both responses.

Gendun Chopel therefore seems to have felt a literary obligation to study Sanskrit erotica. His references to Sanskrit erotica—not just the famous *Kāmasūtra* but other, more obscure works—suggest that he made a diligent study of Sanskrit works. He lists eight by name and says that, "when the long and short ones are added up, there are a little more than thirty" (modern scholarship has identified more than ninety); he does not mention Surūpa's text. Four Sanskrit works on erotica had been translated into English when Gendun Chopel wrote his text: the *Kāmasūtra*, the *Ratiratnapradīpikā*, the *Anaṅgaraṅga*, and the *Ratiśāstra*. However, at this early point of his time in India; it is likely that his ability to read Sanskrit was better than his ability to read English.

It is also the case that Gendun Chopel took especial pride in his knowledge of Sanskrit (and Pāli), confident that it exceeded that of his compatriots. In his colophon to his translation from the Pāli of the *Dhammapada*, he wrote, describing himself:

They say that today there is in Magadha
After a gap of eight hundred years in India,
A late-coming translator [from Tibet]
Who actually reads the Sanskrit treatises.[43]

Thus, one, among several, motivations for his composition of *A Treatise on Passion* was to demonstrate to his Tibetan audience his knowledge of Sanskrit belles lettres and to compose a Tibetan work in that genre. Gendun Chopel decided, therefore, not to translate the *Kāmasūtra* (or another Indian text) but to write his own *Kāmaśāstra*.

Here the literary genre was in some ways as important as the subject matter. Tibetan texts often have a two-part title, a topical title that identifies the subject matter and an ornamental title by which the work is often known. Thus, in the case of Gendun Chopel's magnum opus, the full title of the work is literally translated as *Tales of a Cosmopolitan Traveler, Grains of Gold* (*Rgyal khams rig pas bskor ba'i gtam rgyud gser gyi thang ma*). We note here, however, that Gendun Chopel is presenting his work on erotica as if it were a translation of a Sanskrit text, calling it simply *Kāmaśāstra*. Not only does he not provide an ornamental title, he names his text after an entire genre of Sanskrit literature.

One of Gendun Chopel's purposes in writing *A Treatise on*

Passion, therefore, was to present to his compatriots a largely unknown genre of Sanskrit literature. Much of the more formulaic parts of his text, such as classifications of males and females—where, as in other cultures, there appears to be an inverse proportion between penis length and vaginal depth on the one hand and intelligence and grace on the other—derive from his studies of Indian erotica. Others seem to derive from the folklore of colonial India, such as the rather unflattering description of the sexual practices of women "from the Western lands" (172–74), who are known, he reports, as "semen drinkers." The sections of his text that are derived directly from Sanskrit *kāmaśāstra* works are reproduced rather mechanically, often with a disclaimer at the end. These include sections on moleosophy (the study of moles), predictions made based on the date of the loss of virginity, and the sexual proclivities of women of the different regions of India. There are also sections of his text that derive from what might be called "folk medicine." This is evident, for example, in the section on pregnancy and childbirth, where he stresses the importance of the presence of an experienced woman, while recommending that the room be fumigated with the skin of a black snake to induce dilation.

Although Gendun Chopel states that, among the works of Sanskrit erotica that he studied, he relied most on Vātsyāyana's *Kāmasūtra*, his use of that classic is quite selective. As Alain Daniélou notes in the introduction to his translation, the *Kāmasūtra* is not a sex manual but, rather, is "a picture of the art of living for the civilized and refined citizen."[44] Its context is the "group of three" (*trivarga*): *kāma* (pleasure), *artha* (prosperity), and *dharma* (duty); these would later be expanded to the "four aims of man" (*puruṣārtha*), with *mokṣa* (liberation) added as the fourth. In this sense, the *Kāmasūtra* takes its place with the other famous expositions of the other two of the "group of three," the *Arthaśāstra* of Kautilya and the *Dharmaśāstra* ascribed to Manu, while also incorporating much of their subject matter. Indeed, the opening stanza of the *Kāmasūtra* reads, "We bow down to religion [*dharma*], power [*artha*], and pleasure, because they are the subject of this text."[45] Vātysāyana thus devotes entire chapters to the proper conduct of the gentleman, the use of go-betweens, the various means of acquiring a wife, the proper relationship between the chief wife and secondary wives, and the business practices of the courtesan. None of these, all of which would have been quite foreign to Gendun Chopel's Tibetan readers, is mentioned in his *Treatise on Passion*. He draws most heavily only on the second part (on sex) of the seven parts of Vātsyāyana's text. And even here, Gendun Chopel makes no mention of gay sex. Whether he omitted this with his Tibetan audience in mind is unclear.

It is possible that some of the inspiration for Gendun Chopel's text came not from Indian literature but from Indian art, especially the famous erotic sculpture of Hindu temples such as Khajuraho. In his *Grains of Gold*, he says that the Sun Temple in Konark in Orissa "has the most amazing stone carvings; the temple is covered with about ten thousand stone images of various kinds—from the size of a human to the size of a finger—of men and women in sexual intercourse. Even the ends of the gutters are made in the shape of male and female organs. It is said that if one sees some of the forms of the different ways of love-making depicted on the *paṭa* [friezes] and the *padmaraka* [decorative panels], one's semen will fall on the ground."[46]

Gendun Chopel was aware that one work on Indian erotica had been composed in Tibet and in Tibetan, fifty years earlier. It was by the great scholar of Gendun Chopel's natal Nyingma sect, Ju Mi pham (1846–1912). It was composed in 1886 and was entitled *Treatise on Passion: A Treasure Pleasing to the Entire World* (*'Dod pa'i bstan bcos 'jig rten kun tu dga' ba'i gter*). Here, each of the sixty-four arts of love is clearly enumerated (as they are not so clearly identified in Gendun Chopel's text), eight varieties of each of the eight activities of embracing, kissing, scratching, biting, intercourse, moaning, massaging, and role reversal. Written in a somewhat formal style, and with no apparent erotic experience, Mi pham's text lacks the provocative energy that has aroused readers of Gendun Chopel's *A Treatise on Passion*.[47]

As we shall see below, Gendun Chopel praises his own treatise on passion over that of the monk Mi pham. But Gendun Chopel owes Mi pham an important debt, one that he does not acknowledge. At the end of his work, Mi pham explains his motivation:

From one hundred thousand treatises on passion
Of the sage Svārāyaṇa,
Nāgārjuna gathered a thousand.
Their meaning was summarized by Surūpa, and so on.

From treatises, tantras, and commentaries,
Which are like the various rivers,
This moon is the essence of their collected meaning,
To expand the ocean of happiness
Of beings endowed with passion,
And to illuminate the light of wisdom
Of those endowed with yoga.

To supplement the tantric commentaries,
I have augmented them with a few clear terms.
Because it was not widely known in the past,
And seeing those of the Land of Snows trapped in doubts,
I clearly explained this system [of passion]
Through the power of my intellect.
Because it is adorned by instructions on the profound,

This treatise on passion is better than the others
For those who have a taste for all the pleasures of the world
And for those who have the treasures of attainment.[48]

Vātsyāyana's *Kāmasūtra* and most of the other works of Sanskrit erotica are not presented in a particularly religious context, nor do they claim particular spiritual benefits from the practice of the arts of love. Mi pham, however, as Gendun Chopel would after him, extends the boundaries of passion to include tantric bliss. Another of Gendun Chopel's motivations, therefore, in composing his own treatise on passion is to explore the uses of sexual pleasure as a means of generating, sustaining, and enhancing the bliss necessary for the achievement of the deepest states of realization. His presentation of this topic, however, is not systematic, appearing rather randomly and enigmatically throughout the text, occurring at the very beginning and especially at the end, where he pays homage to "the god of self-arisen bliss." Sexual climax is where duality ceases, where one merges with the other, and the consciousness of separateness is eclipsed. As noted above, in Highest Yoga Tantra, progressive levels of sexual bliss are correlated with progressive levels of realization, leading to the disappearance of dualistic consciousness and the merging of bliss and emptiness, with enlightenment conceived as an orgiastic nondual state.

To readers unaware of the vocabulary of the Vajrayāna, Gendun Chopel's allusions would remain largely invisible. This is clearly intentional on his part; there is a long tradition in tantric literature of using so-called coded language. However, the more interesting, and for Gendun Chopel, the more powerful point, is the immanence of the ultimate in the conventional, that something as common as copulation is, when properly understood, the very path to the profound. As Saraha writes in his *Dohākoṣagīti*, "Although they talk about it in homes here and there, no one understands the nature of great bliss."[49] In general, among the several registers of tantric rhetoric, here Gendun Chopel draws especially from the *sahaja* or "innate" tradition of India and the "great completeness" (*rdzogs chen*) tradition of Tibet, where the natural and spontaneous is valued over the acquired and the deliberate in characterizing the nature of sexual pleasure. In the *Treatise*, Gendun Chopel refers to this innate nature of bliss as "self-arisen" (*rang 'byung*), characterized by naturalness, absence of contrivance, and spontaneity.

301. Spontaneous bliss is uncontrived and self-arisen,
Yet the entire world wears a mask of artifice.
Thus, at the time of delight
A man and woman must shun all customs and facade.

And:

469. The emerging essence made from one's own indestructible elements,
This honey-like taste born from one's own self-arisen body,
Experienced through the hundred thousand pores,
This is something not tasted even by the tongue of the gods in heaven.

Similarly:

559. You appear to nonmeditators and to the mind of a fool.
You befriend all and all are your friend.
Seen by all, yet understood by none,
I bow down to you, god of self-arisen pleasure.

Another of Gendun Chopel's motivations for composing his own treatise on passion is made clear toward the end of the text, where his single mention of Mi pham occurs. He writes:

583. The monk Mi pham wrote from reading.
The wanton Chopel wrote from experience.
The difference in their power to grant blessings,
A passionate man and woman will know through practice.

Thus, another source for *A Treatise on Passion*—a source, which, he proudly announces, he used and Mi pham did not—was his own sexual experience. Gendun Chopel became a Buddhist monk and took the vow of celibacy at an early age. We have little reliable information about his life before he came to Lhasa in 1927, but we can assume that he kept his monastic vows; in a poem written after he left Labrang he contrasts himself with "impure monks."[50]

We know nothing about the loss of his monastic vows or his subsequent sexual life beyond what can be inferred from *A Treatise on Passion* and from a few poems. By the time Gendun Chopel composed *A Treatise on Passion*, he had obviously given up his monastic vows. However, it is unclear when he did so. A friend who saw him prior to his departure for India reports that he was not wearing his monk's robes.[51] This could suggest that he had renounced his monkhood prior to leaving Tibet. The photograph of him taken shortly after he arrived in India (which he sent to his mother) also shows him in lay dress, as do the photos taken on a brief expedition back to Tibet with Rahul Sankrityayan (again, in search of Sanskrit manuscripts) in 1938, the year that he completed *A Treatise on Passion*. During his visit to Sri Lanka in 1940–41, he was photographed wearing the robes of a Theravāda monk, but a poem from that period makes it clear that he was no longer a monk and had not been for some time.

Although the dress of a monk has long disappeared
And the practice of monastic discipline has left no trace,
This meeting with the assembly of elder monks
Must be the fruit of a deed in a former life.[52]

In another poem, he writes that "the unwanted tax of the monk's robe is left in the ashes."[53] He seems never to have married, writing in another poem, "In my youth, I did not take a delightful bride."[54] Yet it is clear that during his time in South Asia, he had an active erotic life, both from what he says himself in *A Treatise on Passion* and what his friends reported in the many stories that are told about him.[55] During a number of his years in India, it was his custom to spend the hot summer months in the Himalayan foothills in Darjeeling and Kalimpong, moving south in the winter sometimes to travel around India, sometimes to work in Calcutta. Working at the Maha Bodhi Society by day, he seems to have frequented the brothels of Calcutta by night.

Upon his return to Tibet, he told of visiting a Japanese woman. After making love and drinking together, he was surprised when she stood up and removed a sheath filled with his semen. He thought to himself, "How sad. She and I never actually touched each other."[56] He also seems to have had a number of love affairs. In a poem written about his time in India, he writes:

Wandering like a deer from the realm of six ranges
To arrive in a distant kingdom of unfamiliar humans,
There I lost my heart to a glamorous fickle woman.
A wretched son who has forgotten his kind parents, I am sad.[57]

However, the most extensive evidence of his erotic life occurs in *A Treatise on Passion*, where we find the exuberance of a young man discovering the joys of sex, made all the more intense because they had been forbidden to him for so long. For the modern reader, these are among the most powerful passages in the work and are the places where we recognize Gendun Chopel's voice, a voice with tints of irony, self-deprecating wit, and a love of women, not merely as sources of male pleasure but as full partners in the play of passion. Thus, we find, at various points throughout the text, a voice very different from the rather formulaic enumeration of body types, regional differences, horoscopes for the loss of virginity, and the best sexual positions for having sons rather than daughters. We find instead a voice that is at once profound and playful:

73. A man and woman, though bereft of wealth and power,
Find the bliss of heaven in their bed.
Even an old man, with hair whiter than a conch,
Finds inexpressible joy in the womb of his old wife.

Although women are said to have enjoyed a higher social status in Tibet than they did in India, when Buddhism was imported from India to Tibet, many of the misogynic aspects of Indian Buddhism came with it, as texts that described the foulness of the female body and that included the prayer that all women be reborn as men were translated from Sanskrit into Tibetan. One of the common words for "woman" in Tibetan is *skyes dman,* literally, "one of inferior birth." It is in this context that Gendun Chopel's condemnation of the way that brahmins treat their wives, his mocking of double standards of promiscuity, and his commitment to female sexual satisfaction are particularly striking.

117. There are also some rules that say
That because a widow is unclean
One should not eat food prepared by her.
This is a saying of heartless brahmins.

118. In ancient times in the land of India, when their husbands died
Women would jump into the flames and die.
If she could not kill herself, though living, she would be considered a corpse.
This is the source of the idea that a widow is polluting.

123. The followers of master Bābhravya say
That there is no fault in having sex with any woman
Except the wife of a brahmin or one's guru.
This is a shameless lie and deception.
Most of the authors of the ancient treatises were brahmins;
They always wrote things like this.

However, Gendun Chopel's concern for women extends beyond his condemnation of hidebound brahmins. He describes the sexual anatomy of males and females at some length, concluding, "There is nothing that a male body has / That women do not also possess" (165). Furthermore, his discussion of female anatomy and sexuality does not derive merely from materia medica; much of what he reports comes from what women have told him. This is particularly evident in the age-old question of whether women ejaculate, where he compares what is said in the texts with what women would (or would not) tell him:

195. Because I like to talk about what lies below the waist,
I have asked many of my female friends about this.
Other than scornful laughs and being hit with fists,
I could not find even one who would give an honest answer.

His dedication to the sexual pleasure of women begins with a concern for their sexual pain; noting that the first sexual intercourse can be painful for a woman, he offers instructions on how to make love without causing pain (126–29). He devotes much more attention, however, to means to produce, sustain, and heighten the sexual pleasure of his female partner, suggesting the apparently universal technique of delaying male orgasm through doing the multiplication tables, as well as the advanced tantric methods of "holding and spreading" described above. Along the way, he prescribes all manner of foreplay, means of transporting both partners into a state of blissful intoxication.

343. Performing in every way
Their favorite postures of passion,
They come to know all the pleasures
Set forth in the treatises.

344. Close, trusting, free of worry,
When both are drunk with deep desire,
What would they not do when making love?
They do everything; they leave nothing.

We thus see many motivations in Gendun Chopel's text. He wants to portray himself as a man of letters, composing a work in Tibetan in the highly cultured genre of Sanskrit erotica. He is the iconoclast and libertine, flaunting his newfound sexual freedom in the face of the staid aristocrats of Lhasa. He is the tantric yogin, demonstrating his penetration of the profound states of sexual yoga. He is the protofeminist, condemning the oppression of woman in traditional South Asian societies and offering techniques for pleasure to both men and women. He insists again and again on the sexual satisfaction of women, urging sexual partners to become expert in the arts of love, not for their own pleasure but for the pleasure of their lovers. And he is that lover, his poetry rising to the rhapsodic when he seeks to express the experience, rather than merely the expertise, of passion.

However, there is something more. Gendun Chopel is often called a "modernist," a term that does and does not accurately describe his many roles in the narrative of the history of Tibet and of Tibetan Buddhism. The complications of that designation are evident in *A Treatise on Passion*, where within a single work he shifts back and forth among many voices, sometimes his own, sometimes the voice of others. Among the most powerful of those voices, and one that is clearly very much his own, is that of what might be called a Marxist sexologist, promoting a populist poetics of sexual pleasure.

We noted above how the Indian erotica of works like the *Kāmasūtra* came to be appropriated by Hindu and Buddhist tantric practitioners, where techniques for mundane pleasure became pathways to supermundane states. In both cases, however, this was a world of elites. The *kāmaśāstra* genre was intended for the cultured gentleman; tantric literature was intended for the spiritually advanced, even if they assumed the guise of the low caste. And whether intended for the cultured gentleman or the tantric yogin, the instructions were provided for men. In the *Treatise on Passion*, Gendun Chopel seeks to wrest the erotic from the elite and give it to the people, of all genders. He does this in two ways.

First, he offers a scathing critique of the culture of celibacy and those who seek to enforce it, that is, the very Buddhist monastic community of which he had so recently been a member. As we saw above, Buddhism is a system in which the monastic code is in many ways imposed on the laity; the devout Buddhist layperson, for example, is encouraged to observe a modified version of the monastic vows every fortnight. In the case of sexuality, what is being prohibited are not only acts that are seen as socially unacceptable but also acts that are seen as indulgences in desire. As a tradition that relies on the laity for its sustenance, celibacy cannot be required, but, stopping short of that, many elements of erotic life are condemned. Thus, the monastic institution seeks to control the means of reproduction, restricting the partner, the time (of both the month and the day), the place, the position, and the orifice where sexual activity could occur. Giving free rein to his storied sense of irony, Gendun Chopel mocks this as hypocritical; the guardians of celibacy condemn by day what they themselves do by night. It is not simply that there could be no Buddhist monks if there were no sexual intercourse, as he also notes. Gendun Chopel sees a real repression at work.

85. When suitable deeds are prohibited in public,
Unsuitable deeds will be done in private.
How can religious and secular laws
Suppress this natural desire of the humans?

And so he calls for the means of reproduction, and of the production of pleasure, to be taken from the elite and distributed freely among the people. He does not call for a simple transfer of the means of pleasure from one elite group to another. Tantric yogins have available to them advanced techniques for reaching the most sublime states of consciousness. The workers of the world only have sex. Orgasm, then, is a human right, one that must not be restricted by institutions of power. Sexual satisfaction must be available equally to all. It is important to note that he is not demanding that all partake; he acknowledges that there are many, including Buddhist monks, who should not read his book.

Thus, in addition to reading *A Treatise on Passion* as inspired by Sanskrit belles lettres, as yet another attempt to be shocking by the great iconoclast of modern Tibet, and as coded instructions for the attainment of tantric bliss, Gendun Chopel's ode to orgasm might also be read as a product of its time: the last days of the great sexologists, figures like Havelock Ellis, Sigmund Freud, and his renegade disciple, Wilhelm Reich. They were the prophets of what Foucault called "the repressive hypothesis." In the late nineteenth and early twentieth centuries, these and other figures were "subtle theologians," who "chastised the old order, denounced hypocrisy, and praised the rights of the immediate and the real."[58] The effects of the repression of sex is of course a central theme throughout Freud's substantial oeuvre; he devotes one of his most famous essays, *Civilization and Its Discontents*, to the topic of sublimation. There, he explains that "civilization is obeying the laws of economic necessity, since a large amount of the psychical energy which it uses for its own purposes has to be withdrawn from sexuality. In this respect civilization behaves towards sexuality as a people or a stratum of its population does which has subjected another one to its exploitation. Fear of a revolt by the suppressed elements drives it to stricter precautionary measures."[59] Wilhelm Reich would go further, declaring that "the disturbances of genital functioning . . . are the direct cause of all forms of psychic illness, including psychosis, perversion, and neurotic criminality."[60] He also ascribed a range of physical illnesses, including various heart ailments, to what he called "sexual stasis." The suppression of genital gratification for Reich had larger social consequences: "We must assume that the general cultural negation of sexuality and the tendency to fragment and suppress it has played a decisive role in the emergence of human sadism."[61] Like Gendun Chopel, Reich was committed to the sexual health of the working classes, offering free counseling at clinics in Vienna and Berlin.[62]

It is unclear whether Gendun Chopel read authors like Marx and Freud. There is no mention of them in his extant writings; in *Grains of Gold*, he mentions Darwin at one point. It is the case, however, that Gendun Chopel spent much time with Bengali intellectuals, including Rahul Sankrityayan (a committed Marxist who visited the Soviet Union) and his circle. He also spent time with the Roerich family, important figures in the Russian avant garde and committed Theosophists. It is therefore possible that some of his thinking about sexuality was influenced by his conversations with such figures. It is certainly the case, however, that a number of passages in the *Treatise on Passion* resonate with the repressive hypothesis; Gendun Chopel uses the text, "to speak out against the powers that be, to utter truths and promise bliss, to link together enlightenment, liberation, and manifold pleasures; to pronounce a discourse that combines the fervor of knowledge, the determination to change the laws, and the longing for the garden of earthly delights."[63]

Gendun Chopel, however, was first and foremost a Tibetan, and so he offers not a garden but a peak. He presents his book as an offering to all, male and female, young and old. It is a book that is both meant to arouse passion and then to direct that passion to orgasm, a human right. He charts the pathways to what he calls the sixteen peaks of pleasure.

Gendun Chopel is also a Buddhist: an incarnate lama of the Nyingma sect, a former monk and *geshe* (without having received the title) of the Geluk sect, a consummate scholar of the vast canons of Tibetan Buddhist literature. His enemies would condemn him as an atheist and a communist, yet one need only read his works to dismiss such charges; he remained a devout Buddhist throughout his life. Still, his relationship to Buddhism, and its institutions, was complex, and that complexity is perhaps nowhere more evident than in *A Treatise on Passion*. Here he repeatedly debunks the insistence on celibacy—and its repressive culture—that provides the foundation for Buddhist monasticism, with full knowledge of the traditional view that where there are no monks there is no Buddhism. At the same time, he never seems to question one of the foundations of Buddhist tantrism: that enlightenment is attained through the practice of sexual yoga. Indeed, as we have seen, he laces the language of tantric sex throughout his treatise. In this regard, he is devout, never seeming to doubt that sex leads to enlightenment. Where we see contradictions, perhaps he saw none: he could be at once a leader of the revolution against sexual repression and misogyny and also be (or aspire to be) a tantric yogin, in sexual union with his consort, seeking the union of bliss and emptiness.

Indeed, despite its lack of an ornamental title, *A Treatise on Passion* carries many of the marks of a traditional Tibetan Buddhist text. For example, it begins with an expression of worship (*mchod brjod*), with Gendun Chopel paying homage to the innate reality of *mahāmudrā* and the sixteen types of bliss of the *Kāla-*

cakra Tantra before praising the divine lovers of the Hindu pantheon, Śiva (called Maheśvara here) and Parvatī (called Gaurī). And he closes the text with a dedication of merit, or perhaps a parody of the traditional Buddhist dedication of merit, offering the merit of composing his text not to the welfare of all sentient beings, but to his lovers, three in particular, judging by their names, a Buddhist, a Hindu, and a Muslim. Yet the closing stanzas also express Gendun Chopel's vaster aspirations for his treatise and capture what is perhaps the central motivation for this work. It is his prayer that all humans achieve a different kind of bliss.

586. Through this virtue [of writing this], may all like-minded friends
Cross the dark road of misty desires
And see the sky of the true nature of reality
From the summit of the sixteen peaks of pleasure.

587. Yudön, Gangā, Asali, and the others,
The women who joined with my body,
May they persist on the path, from bliss to bliss,
To arrive at great bliss, the place of *dharmakāya*.

588. May all humble people who live on this broad earth
Be delivered from the pit of merciless laws
And be able to indulge, with freedom,
In common enjoyments, so needed and right.

A TREATISE ON PASSION AS A WORK OF POETRY

Since the thirteenth century, the basic unit of the Tibetan poem has been the four-line stanza, the Tibetan version of the Sanskrit *śloka*. In Sanskrit, the *śloka* was composed of thirty-two syllables, commonly in two lines of an equal number of syllables. Each line was divided into two feet (*pāda*), also of an equal number of syllables; feet were often of eight syllables, lines of sixteen. In the royal Tibetan translation academies, where Sanskrit Buddhist texts were rendered into Tibetan, the standard practice was to give a full line to each of the four feet of the Sanskrit original; what was two lines in Sanskrit would be rendered in four in Tibetan. Each of the four lines was of an equal number of syllables. This would become the most common form of Tibetan poetry.

Tibetan is an alphabetic language, with letters forming syllables, each of which is separated by a dot. Each syllable carries some meaning, either as a word itself or as a grammatical marker. Words are typically one, two, or three syllables, usually two, the first of which is accented. Some ancient Tibetan songs had lines of six syllables each, but beginning from the Buddhist period, the lines are most often of an odd number, usually seven or nine, but sometimes as long as twenty-three. The standard meter was trochaic. Within this basic structure, Tibetan poets crafted their own embellishments, such as starting each line with the same syllable, repeating the same syllable in each line, as well as various forms of alliteration, assonance, consonance, and word play. Gendun Chopel was considered to be a master of all these forms, composing poems that displayed a high level of technical skill but that remained at once elegant and earthy. He most often wrote nine-syllable verses but ranged from as short as seven or eight to as long as eleven or fifteen.

Like many great poets, Gendun Chopel was also a connoisseur of Tibetan poetry. One of his biographers reports that Gendun Chopel would recite verses from Sakya Paṇḍita, Tsong kha pa, Khedrup Gelek Palsang, Shangshung Chöwang Drakpa, and the First and the Seventh Dalai Lamas.[64] Reciting from Tsong kha pa's *Ocean of Clouds*, a hymn to the bodhisattva of wisdom Mañjuśrī, or the First Dalai Lama's *Hymns to Goddess Tārā*, Gendun

Chopel would say, "This is what poetry should look like." For majesty of style Gendun Chopel particularly admired the poetry of the Fifth Dalai Lama, saying, "It would be difficult for anyone else to achieve the effect he produces with his fierce poems and reprimands."[65]

Gendun Chopel is renowned as the greatest Tibetan poet of the twentieth century, and *A Treatise on Passion* is his longest and perhaps his most famous poem. The entire work—apart from a few interspersed prose remarks that function almost as footnotes—is composed in perfectly metered verse. Many passages flow with effortless fluidity and evocative power. Some verses, such as the following, are composed in such a way that they echo in a Tibetan reader's mind like a memorable melody:

4. This Realm of Desire is the place of passion;
All its creatures seek passion.
The most perfect of all pleasures of passion
Is the bliss of sexual passion of a man and a woman.

Tibetans regard Gendun Chopel as a consummate master of the poetic form; as they would put it, words melt in his hands like butter, which he then shapes into anything he wishes. His poems are particularly noted for their immediacy and ease, with what is called "natural expression" (*rang bzhin bjod pa'i rgyan*), without the embellishments of complex layers of metaphor.[66]

When looked at, the marvels of the world seem pleasing,
When attained, each has its own suffering.
After moments of brief happiness become but a dream,
There is always something that makes me sad.[67]

Gendun Chopel is also renowned for his use of irony, one of the nine moods (*rasa*) of the classical Indian poetics.[68] It is much in evidence in *A Treatise of Passion.*

76. A beggar may turn up his nose at gold.
A hungry guest may spit at his meal.
Though everyone condemns sex with their mouth,
Just this is the place of pleasure in their mind.

78. Whatever miracles that occur on earth are done by humans.
Humans are produced by sex between a man and a woman.
When considered this way, what deed has greater meaning
Than the union of the two organs?

79. For a deed of such great importance,
There is no need to be exhorted to struggle.
All men and women do this naturally.
This is the law set forth by the king, dependent origination.

Among the classical Indian poets, Tibetans writers often celebrate Daṇḍin, whose *Mirror of Poetry* (*Kāvyādarśa*) shaped classical Tibetan poetry. Gendun Chopel knew the *Mirror of Poetry* well, studying it in his youth and apparently making his own translation from the Sanskrit when he was in India. He considered Mi pham's commentary on Daṇḍin's treatise to be among the best. During his time in India, Gendun Chopel's poetry was strongly influenced by this study of other Sanskrit poets, none more than Kālidāsa. His *Cloud Messenger* (*Meghadūta*) was already known in Tibetan. In India, Gendun Chopel encountered his other works and seems to have been immediately inspired. In a letter written to Rahul Sankrityayan in February 1936, he says that his greatest wish is to translate *Śakuntalā* into Tibetan; he would eventually make a partial translation. He even expressed the mildly heretical view that Kālidāsa (a Hindu) was a greater poet than Aśvaghoṣa (a Buddhist). Writing in *Grains of Gold* he asserted: "Some impartial people say that he was not greater than Aśvaghoṣa, but because Aśvaghoṣa wrote poems about religious matters, he did not conform to the mentality of the common people, while he [Kālidāsa] wrote about ordinary events of the world, thus captivating everyone."[69] Kālidāsa was famed for his long lines; we can observe that influence in this verse by Gendun Chopel:

To the sharp weapons of the demons, you offered delicate
flowers in return.
When the enraged Devadatta pushed down a boulder [to kill
you], you practiced silence.
Son of Śakyas, incapable of casting even an angry glance at your
enemy,
What intelligent person would honor you as a friend for
protection from the great enemy, fearful saṃsāra?[70]

Although he was deeply versed in Sanskrit poetics, Gendun Chopel often eschewed its conventions in his own poems, especially the embellishments for which Sanskrit *kāvya* is so famous, especially the synonyms, in which clouds are "elephants" and the sky is the "path of the gods." He felt that the best poetry was like speech without superfluous words and should be something that can be understood on its first reading.[71]

Like Kālidāsa, Gendun Chopel's poetry has a sense of natural ease, far different from the somewhat contrived style that was fashionable among Tibetan authors who celebrated what they regarded as high literature. At times, his poetry has something of the folk style of the Sixth Dalai Lama: easily approachable, with metaphors immediately familiar to ordinary Tibetans. Like the poems of the Sixth Dalai Lama, and to some extent, the Seventh Dalai Lama as well, his poems display the tremendous sense of freedom, flexibility, and fluidity of the Tibetan language. These are the qualities that appear throughout *A Treatise on Passion.*

A hallmark of Gendun Chopel's poetry is his ability to create combinations of words that create an immediate poetic effect. He will often repeat a specific word or a grammatical particle in successive lines, at exactly the same place in the line, even when expressing contrast. We can see this clearly in the following stanza:

554. Each step we take is for the sake of pleasure.
Each word we speak is for the sake of pleasure.
Good deeds are done for the sake of pleasure.
Bad deeds are done for the sake of pleasure.

He repeats the same word "each" (in Tibetan, the verb followed by the particle *yang*) at exactly the same spot in the first two lines, immediately creating a lyrical sense to the lines, making the contrast of virtues and sins in the next two lines more striking. He then increases the impact of the verse by expanding the frame in the next stanza:

555. The eyeless ant runs for the sake of pleasure.
The legless worm crawls for the sake of pleasure.
In brief, all the world is racing with each other,
Running toward pleasure, one faster than the next.

The previous verse, with its reference to virtuous and sinful deeds, causes the reader to assume that he is describing the human realm. However, Gendun Chopel is making a stronger claim here, that the pursuit of pleasure drives all beings. The imagery of blind ants and crawling worms graphically makes his point.

In the Tibetan community, *A Treatise on Passion* has remained the most widely read and admired of Gendun Chopel's many works. Today, if one asks educated Tibetans of the younger generation about Gendun Chopel and his writings, most will immediately mention his *Treatise on Passion* and his unfinished history of imperial Tibet, *The White Annals*. A scholar will know his other works as well, especially his *Grains of Gold: Tales of a Cos-*

mopolitan Traveler, his editing of Tibetan historical annals from Dunhuang, and his memorable poetry. Although much of the popularity of Gendun Chopel's *Treatise on Passion* is due to its subject matter, the beauty of its poetry is also responsible for Tibetans' fondness for this text. In the early eighteenth century, the Sixth Dalai Lama offered his people a treasury of love songs, used by generations of Tibetans to express their love to each other. In the twentieth century, Gendun Chopel completed what the Sixth Dalai Lama had begun, empowering the ordinary person to partake in the celebration of sexuality.

ABOUT THE TRANSLATION

There are always special challenges in translating poetry. In Tibetan, the immediate issues are line length and meter. Tibetan poems do not rhyme. Instead, each line has the same number of syllables. One of the challenges for the translator, therefore, is not rhyme but line length, seeking to provide a translation in four lines of at least roughly the same number of syllables. Under these constraints, word choice becomes not only a matter of denotation, connotation, and euphony but also length. This becomes a particular problem when translating Buddhist poetry (which constitutes the great majority of Tibetan poetry), where English tends toward words of Greek and Latin etymology for religious terminology and, hence, words of multiple syllables.

A similar problem faces the translator of erotica. English has a rich selection of one-syllable words for the male and female genitalia. But those words, even today, are rarely spoken in polite company. Read on a page, and perhaps especially in a poem, they stop the reader. Such a pause becomes extended in a translation of a poem. Did the original use vulgar language? The English alternative falls at the other end of the spectrum: the clinical, where the vocabulary is used largely in a medical context. Such words are hardly erotic, and for the Tibetan translator they have the additional disadvantage of having many syllables. English thus seems strangely impoverished for the translation of erotica.

When one turns to the Tibetan, the situation is not very different. The standard terms for vagina would be literally translated as "female sign" (*mo mtshan*), "birth door" (*skye sgo*), and "birth place" (*skyes gnas*). The standard word for penis is "male sign" (*pho mtshan*). Gendun Chopel uses these words at times, especially in the more anatomical sections of the work. However, when describing lovemaking, he does not use Tibetan, instead transliterating the standard Sanskrit terms: *bhaga* for vagina and *liṅga* for penis. His more literate Tibetan readers would know what they mean. His less learned readers could easily guess. His choice moves the terms away from both the vulgar and the clinical into a more shaded realm of the erotic, where he then describes the acts of love in vivid detail.

A Treatise on Passion was not published during Gendun Chopel's lifetime, circulating only in manuscript form. In her biography of Gendun Chopel, Heather Stoddard reports that Gendun Chopel sent the manuscript to the aristocrat Kashöpa (1903–86). It was not published until 1967, by Dhongthog Tenpai Gyaltsen, from a manuscript that had belonged to the renowned Nyingma hierarch, Dudjom Rinpoche (1904–87).[72] Dhongthog brought out a second edition, printed in New Delhi in 1969, which he reports was based on a manuscript that had belonged to Gendun Chopel. That edition also includes Mi pham's *Treatise on Passion*. In 1983, the Tibetan Cultural Printing Press in Dharamsala produced a modern typeset edition of Gendun Chopel's *Treatise*, also accompanied by Mi pham's text, likely based on Dhongthog's edition. This Dharamsala edition became the basis for a somewhat strange modern edition, with illustrations and references to modern sexology, published by Tenzin Norbu in Sarnath, in 2006.

It is noteworthy that when Gendun Chopel's works were first collected by his student Horkhang and published in three volumes in 1990, *A Treatise on Passion* was not included. However, when his collected works were published in five volumes by Zhangkar Gyiling Press in Hong Kong in 2006, the text was included in the final volume. Unfortunately, the Tibetan editors of his collected works do not provide any information on which manuscript they based their version on.

In preparing the translation, we made use of four editions of the text: (1) *'Dod pa'i bstan bcos*, edited by T. G. Dhongthog (1967; rev., Delhi: T. G. Dhongthog Rinpoche, 1969); (2) *'Dod pa'i bstan bcos* (Dharamsala: Tibetan Cultural Printing Press, 1983); (3) *'Dod pa'i bstan bcos* in *'Dzam gling rig pa'i dpa' bo mkhas dbang dge 'dun chos 'phel gyi gsung 'bum*, vol. 5 (Hong Kong: Zhang kang gyi ling dpe skrun khang, 2006), 1–72; and (4) *'Dod pa'i bstan bcos*, edited by Tenzin Norbu (Sarnath: Mani Publication, 2005). Because it is the most readily available version, we have provided the page numbers of the Tibetan text in Gendun Chopel's five-volume collected works (no. 3 above) in brackets in the body of the text.

None of the Tibetan editions have been prepared in what could be called a critical edition, with comments on differences in chapter divisions, verse numbering, or annotations of variant readings. Indeed, the Tibetan text of *A Treatise on Passion* deserves a critical edition; each of the available editions contains a number of errors, especially in the rendering of Sanskrit terms and names, likely the result of the inability of editors to read Gendun Chopel's transliteration of the Sanskrit. We have attempted to correct these, drawing at times on the efforts of Jeffrey Hopkins in *Tibetan Arts of Love* (Ithaca, NY: Snow Lion

Publications, 1992). In the course of the project, we have been grateful for the assistance of Madhav Deshpande, Carl Ernst, Anna Johnson, Sara McClelland, and Sureel Shah.

Our translation reproduces the text division found in the early Dhongthog edition; it is unclear whether this division existed in the original manuscript or was inserted by a later editor; the text does not contain chapter divisions in the traditional Tibetan sense.

To assist the reader in locating passages, we have numbered all the verses. While most verses have the traditional four-line form, there are cases where the verse runs to six lines. Although we have adopted the topical division of the text found in the Tibetan edition, we have provided a single sequence of verse numbering for the entire text.

Because Gendun Chopel's treatise is composed in perfectly metered verse, we have also chosen to translate it in verse. Although it is impossible to render the Tibetan in metered English, we have attempted to capture something of the spirit and poetic energy of Gendun Chopel's verse. Indeed, our primary motivation for undertaking this translation of *A Treatise on Passion* was to render what is perhaps Gendun Chopel's most famous verse work in verse. In this sense, our translation differs from the prose translation by our friend and teacher Jeffrey Hopkins, published in 1992 as *Tibetan Arts of Love*. In preparing this afterword and translation, we have benefited greatly from his pioneering work.

*

NOTES FOR "BACKGROUND TO *A TREATISE ON PASSION*"

1. For a translation of this poem, see Donald S. Lopez Jr., trans., *In the Forest of Faded Wisdom: 104 Poems by Gendun Chopel* (Chicago: University of Chicago Press, 2009), 64–67.
2. For Gendun Chopel's account of their expedition, including a list of the manuscripts they discovered, see Gendun Chopel, *Grains of Gold: Tales of a Cosmopolitan Traveler*, trans. Thupten Jinpa and Donald S. Lopez Jr. (Chicago: University of Chicago Press, 2014), 29–57.
3. Ibid., 57.
4. For a very useful listing of Gendun Chopel's writings, both published and rumored, see Irmgard Mengele, *dGe-'dun-chos-'phel: A Biography of the 20th Century Tibetan Scholar* (Dharamsala: Library of Tibetan Works and Archives, 1999), 85–113. This should be supplemented by Rdo rje rgyal, ed., *Mkhas dbang dge 'dun chos 'phel gyi gsar rnyed gsung rtsom* (Zi ling: Zi ling mi rigs par khang, 2002), although the attribution to Gendun Chopel of a lengthy pilgrimage guide to India reprinted in this volume is mistaken.
5. The most complete biography of Gendun Chopel remains Heather Stoddard, *Le mendiant de l'Amdo* (Paris: Société d'ethnographie, 1985). Among English-language works, see Mengele, *dGe-'dun-chos-'phel*; and Kyabje Kirti Rinpoche Lobsang Tenzin, *Supplementary Chapters on Gedun Choephel*, trans. Yeshi Dhondup (Kirti Monastery, India: Kirti Jepa Monastery, 2008). For a translation of Gendun Chopel's account of his time in South Asia, see

Gendun Chopel, *Grains of Gold*, 29–57. For the paintings and sketches he produced during his travels, see Donald S. Lopez Jr., *Gendun Chopel: Tibet's First Modern Artist* (New York: Trace Foundation, 2013). For a brief biography and selections from his works, see Donald S. Lopez Jr., *Gendun Chopel: Tibet's Modern Visionary* (Boulder, CO: Shambhala, 2018).

6. A number of works, including those by Lopez, have reported that Gendun Chopel returned to Tibet in 1946. However, a recently discovered letter from Gendun Chopel to the Russian scholar George Roerich indicates that he arrived in the summer of 1945. In a letter dated August 25, 1945, he reports that he is back in Lhasa and that for the past month he has been invited to the homes of a number of aristocrats.
7. Two of Gendun Chopel's disciples wrote important biographies of their teacher. The first, Rakra Tethong Thupten Choedar (Rak ra bkras mthong thub bstan chos dar, 1925–2012), was an incarnate lama who studied at Drepung monastery and later settled in Switzerland. His biography of Gendun Chopel, entitled *Dge 'dun chos 'phel gyi lo rgyus*, written in 1979, was included as the first entry of the five-volume collected works of Gendun Chopel published in 2006 as *'Dzam gling rig pa'i dpa' bo mkhas dbang dge 'dun chos 'phel gyi gsung 'bum* (Hong Kong: Zhang kang gyi ling dpe skrun khang). The second, Lachung Apo (A pho bla chung, also known as Shes rab rgya mtsho, 1905–75), was a Nyingma scholar from the Gojo region of Khams. His biography of Gendun Chopel was first published in 1973 as an entry in Khetsun Sangpo's *Biographical Dictionary of Tibet and Tibetan Buddhism*. For a translation and study of the biography, see Mengele, *dGe-'dun-chos-'phel*.
8. Tibetan historians have been unable to determine the reason (or reasons) for Gendun Chopel's imprisonment. In his preface to the five-volume collected works of Gendun Chopel, the noted Amdo scholar Chukyé Gendun Samten (Chu skyes dge 'dun bsam gtan) writes, "The exact reason why he was imprisoned remains unclear. There seem to be a variety of explanations. Some say that he produced counterfeit currency, some allege he was a spy for a foreign power, and others say it was because of his forceful candor." See *'Dzam gling rig pa'i dpa' bo mkhas dbang dge 'dun chos 'phel gyi gsung 'bum*, 1:6.
9. For a translation, see Donald S. Lopez Jr., *The Madman's Middle Way: Reflections on Reality of the Tibetan Monk Gendun Chopel* (Chicago: University of Chicago Press, 2006).
10. See Gendun Chopel, *In the Forest of Faded Wisdom*, 93.

11. See Agañña Sutta ("Knowledge of Origins") in Maurice Walsh, trans., *The Long Discourses of the Buddha: A Translation of the Dīgha Nikāya* (Boston: Wisdom Publications, 1995), 407–15.
12. Linda Covill, trans., *Handsome Nanda by Aśvaghoṣa*, Clay Sanskrit Library (New York: New York University Press, 2007), 203.
13. There were homosexual relations, both consensual and coerced, among Buddhist monks in Tibet. See, for example, Melvyn C. Goldstein, *The Struggle for Modern Tibet: The Autobiography of Tashi Tsering* (Armonk, NY: M. E. Sharpe, 1997). On homosexuality in Indian Buddhism, see José Ignacio Cabezón, *Sexuality in Classical South Asian Buddhism* (Boston: Wisdom Publications, 2017), 373–451.
14. See Tsong-kha-pa, *The Great Treatise on the Stages of the Path to Enlightenment* (Ithaca, NY: Snow Lion Publications, 2000), 1:220–21.
15. For an example from contemporary Thailand, see Benedict Anderson's *The Fate of Rural Hell: Asceticism and Desire in Rural Thailand* (Kolkata: Seagull Books, 2012).
16. See Claus Vogel, *Surūpa's Kāmaśāstra: An Erotic Treatise in the Tibetan Tanjur*, Studia Orientalia 30.3 (Helsinki: Edidit Societas Orientalis Fennica, 1965), 4n6.
17. See Patrick Olivelle, trans., *Life of the Buddha by Aśvaghoṣa* (New York: New York University Press and JJC Foundation, 2008), 115.
18. The story of Sudinna is drawn from I. B. Horner, trans., *The Book of the Discipline (Vinaya-Piṭaka)*, vol. 1, *Suttavibhaṅga* (London: Luzac & Co., 1949), 21–38.
19. T. W. Rhys Davids, trans., *The Questions of King Milinda*, The Sacred Books of the East, vol.35 (Oxford: Clarendon Press, 1890), 1:237–39.
20. See Thanissaro Bhikkhu, trans., *The Buddhist Monastic Code I*, rev. ed. (Valley Center, CA: Metta Forest Monastery, 1994), 4–5.
21. See Donald S. Lopez Jr., ed., *Buddhist Scriptures* (London: Penguin Books, 2004), 244–45.
22. On Indian Buddhist attitudes toward women and the female body, see Liz Wilson, *Charming Cadavers: Horrific Figurations of the Feminine in Indian Buddhist Hagiographic Literature* (Chicago: University of Chicago Press, 1992). On Indian Buddhist attitudes toward sexuality, see Cabezón, *Sexuality in Classical South Asian Buddhism*.
23. See Jan Nattier, *A Few Good Men: The Bodhisattva Path according to "The Inquiry of Ugra" (Ugraparipṛcchā)* (Honolulu: University of Hawai'i Press, 2003), 315.

24. Ibid., 249–52.
25. See Bernard Faure, *The Red Thread: Buddhist Approaches to Sexuality* (Princeton, NJ: Princeton University Press, 1998), 92.
26. See Mark Tatz, *The Skill in Means Sūtra (Upāyakauśalya)* (Delhi: Motitlal Banarsidass, 1994), 39–45.
27. Ibid., 34–35.
28. Tsong kha pa discusses the bodhisattva vows in his *Byang chub gzhung lam*. For a translation, see Mark Tatz, *Asaṅga's Chapter on Ethics with the Commentary of Tsong kha pa: The Basic Path of Awakening, the Complete Bodhisattva* (Lewiston, NY: Edwin Mellen Press, 1986).
29. One of the earliest and most influential works in this genre of "the three vows" is that by Sakya Paṇḍita. For an English translation, see *A Clear Differentiation of the Three Codes*, trans. Jared Douglas Rhoton (Albany, NY: SUNY Press, 2002). On the topic of the three vows, see Jan-Ulrich Sobisch, *Three Vow Theory in Tibetan Buddhism* (Wiesbaden: Ludwig Reichert Verlag, 2002).
30. On the challenges of how to understand the description of sexual practices in the Buddhist tantras, see David. B. Gray, *The Cakrasamvara Tantra: A Study and Annotated Translation* (New York: American Institute of Buddhist Studies, 2007), 103–31.
31. Works by Tsong kha pa on tantra available in English translation include Jeffery Hopkins, *Tantra in Tibet: The Great Exposition of Secret Mantra* (London: Allen and Unwin, 1977); Tsong kha pa, *A Lamp to Illuminate the Five Stages: Teachings on the Guhyasamāja Tantra*, trans. Gavin Kilty, Library of Tibetan Classics (Boston: Wisdom Publications, 2013); and Thomas F. Yarnall, *Great Treatise on Secret Mantra: Chapters XI–XII (The Creation Stage)* (New York: American Institute of Buddhist Studies, 2013).
32. *Rdo rje mkha' 'gro'i rgyud*, Kangyur D, rgyud ka, 2a6.
33. *Tantrarājaśrīlaghusaṃvara* (*Rgyud kyi rgyal po dpal bde mchog nyung ngu*), Kangyur D, rgyud ka, chap. 29, 203b3.
34. Tsong kha pa, *Rdzogs rim dngos grub snye ma,* Collected Works of Tsong kha pa, Kumbum ed., vol. *dza*, 26b3.
35. See Tsong kha pa, *A Lamp to Illuminate the Five Stages*, 524.
36. *Dpal rdo rje phreng ba mngon par brjod pa*, Kangyur D, rgyud ca, 214b6.
37. See Tsong kha pa, *Rim lnga gdan rdzogs*, Collected Works of Tsong kha pa, Kumbum ed., vol. *nya*, 22a4. See also Tsong kha pa, *A Lamp to Illuminate the Five Stages*, 202–4.
38. For example, a well-known hymn to Tsong kha pa by his disciple Khedrup

Gelek Palsang reads, "When you actualized the *dharmakāya* of clear light / At that point your body turned into a mass of light. / In the intermediate state you attained the illusory body of *sambhogakāya*. / I pray to you who have found the supreme attainment." See Mkhas grub dge legs dpal bzang. *Gsung thor bu* (Miscellaneous Works), Collected Works, Kumbum ed., vol. *ba*, 6a1.

39. See Yael Bentor, "Can Women Attain Enlightenment through Vajrayāna Practice?" in, *Karmic Passages: Israeli Scholarship on India*, ed. David Shulman and Shalva Weil (New Delhi: Oxford University Press, 2008), 123–37. For the experiences of a twentieth-century Tibetan woman in the practice of sexual yoga, see Sarah H. Jacoby, *Love and Liberation: Autobiographical Writings of the Tibetan Buddhist Visionary Sera Khandro* (New York: Columbia University Press, 2014).
40. See Gendun Chopel, *Grains of Gold*, 30.
41. For an edition, translation, and study of this text, see Vogel, *Surūpa's Kāmaśāstra*.
42. See Donald S. Lopez Jr., ed., *Religions of Tibet in Practice* (Princeton, NJ: Princeton University Press, 1997), 381.
43. See Gendun Chopel, *In the Forest of Faded Wisdom*, 77. Describing the Sanskrit compositions of his fellow Tibetans, he writes in a poem:

    From Khagya to Gengya [two places in Amdo] is far.
    The road from Ü to Amdo is very long.
    From Magadha to Tibet is most distant.
    From actual Sanskrit to Tibetanized Sanskrit is farther than that.

    See *In the Forest of Faded Wisdom*, 122–23. The translation of the first line as it appears in *In the Forest of Faded Wisdom* is mistaken, failing to recognize that Kha rgya and Rgan rgya are place names in Amdo.
44. Alain Daniélou, trans., *The Complete Kāma Sūtra* (Rochester, VT: Park Street Press, 1994), 4.
45. Vatsayana Mallanaga, *Kamasutra*, trans. Wendy Doniger and Sudhir Kakar (New York: Oxford University Press, 2002), 1; the Sanskrit terms in brackets have been added. Among the various English translations of the *Kāmasūtra*, that of Doniger and Kakar is considered to be the most accurate.
46. See Gendun Chopel, *Grains of Gold*, 80.
47. On Mi pham's text, see Sarah Jacoby, "The Science of Sexual Pleasure according to a Buddhist Monk: Ju Mipam's Contribution to *Kāmaśāstra* Liter-

ature in Tibet," *Bulletin of the School of Oriental and African Studies* 80, no. 2 (2017) 30.

48. Mi pham rgya mtsho, *'Dod pa'i bstan bcos 'jig rten kun tu dga' ba'i gter* in *The Extended Redaction of the Complete Works of Ju Mi-Pham Series*, vol. 13 (nga) (Paro, Bhutan, 1984–93), 13a6–13b3 (549–50); Tibetan Buddhist Resource Center (TBRC) ID W23468.
49. *Do ha mdzod kyi glu,* Tengyur D, rgyud *wi,* 74a1.
50. See Gendun Chopel, *In the Forest of Faded Wisdom*, 65–67.
51. See Donald S. Lopez Jr., *Gendun Chopel: Tibet's First Modern Artist* (New York: Trace Foundation, 2013), 46.
52. See Gendun Chopel, *In the Forest of Faded Wisdom*, 79.
53. Ibid., 71.
54. Ibid., 93.
55. See, for example, the recollections of Gendun Chopel's sometime traveling companion, Golok Jigme, in director Luc Schaedler's 2005 documentary, *Angry Monk* (New York: First Run Features, 2009).
56. See Kirti rin po che blo bzang bstan 'dzin, ed., *Dge 'dun chos 'phel gyi rab byed zhabs btags ma*, 2nd ed., (Dharamsala, India: Institute of Higher Tibetan Studies, 2003), 245–246.
57. See Gendun Chopel, *In the Forest of Faded Wisdom*, 69.
58. Michel Foucault, *The History of Sexuality: An Introduction* (New York: Vintage Books, 1990), 1:7.
59. Sigmund Freud, *The Standard Edition of the Complete Psychological Works of Sigmund Freud*, trans. by James Strachey (London: Hogarth Press, 1961), 21:104.
60. Wilhelm Reich, *Genitality in the Theory and Therapy of Neurosis*, vol. 2 of *Early Writings*, trans. Philip Schmitz (New York: Farrar Straus Giroux, 1980). This is the second edition of a work first published in 1927 as *Die Funktion des Orgasmus.* In 1942, Reich would publish a kind of scientific autobiography entitled *The Discovery of Orgone*, vol. 1, *The Function of the Orgasm*, later republished as *The Function of the Orgasm: Sex-Economic Problems of Biological Energy*. This was the first of Reich's books to be translated into English and would be his most widely read work. In order to distinguish the 1927 essay from the more famous 1942 work, the translators entitled the work cited here as *Genitality in the Theory and Therapy of Neurosis.*

    There are noteworthy parallels between the lives of Gendun Chopel and William Reich, who were largely contemporaries (Reich was born in 1897 and died in 1957), including their early brilliance, their condemnation for deviations from orthodoxy, their imprisonment on false charges, and their posthumous fame.

61. Reich, *Genitality in the Theory and Therapy of Neurosis*, 177.
62. See Juliet Mitchell, *Psychoanalysis and Feminism: A Radical Reassessment of Freudian Psychoanalysis* (New York: Basic Books, 2000), 138–52.
63. Foucault, *A History of Sexuality*, 7.
64. Rak ra bkras mthong, *Dge 'dun chos 'phel gyi lo rgyus*, 93.
65. Ibid., 94.
66. Jinpa recalls the first time he came across Gendun Chopel's poetry:

> This was around 1979. I was then a young monk studying at the Shartse College of Ganden Monastery in southern India where I was in the *labrang* (house) of Zemey Rinpoché, a noted Tibetan scholar and poet. Rinpoché showed me a handwritten copy of one of Gendun Chopel's most memorable poems, the one that says, "the unwanted tax of the monk's robe is left in the ashes." The widow of the former Tibetan official Zurkhang had come to India to make offerings to the sacred places as well as to the monasteries in honor of her late husband. Both Zurkhang and his wife had known Kyabjé Trijang Rinpoché, the late junior tutor to the Dalai Lama, and were also aware of the kindness with which Trijang Rinpoché had treated Gendun Chopel when the latter was in prison. Gendun Chopel had given a handwritten copy of that poem to Zurkhang, which lady Zurkhang had offered to Trijang Rinpoché. He in turn had lent it to my own teacher Zemey Rinpoché. Showing me this poem, beautifully handwritten on traditional Tibetan paper and folded into a long parchment, Zemey Rinpoché told me that Gendun Chopel's poetry brings out the natural rhythm and elegance of Tibetan.

One should note that in his youth Zemey Rinpoché had written a lengthy and scathing rebuttal of Gendun Chopel's *Adornment for Nāgārjuna's Thought*.

67. Gendun Chopel, *In the Forest of Faded Wisdom*, 70–71.
68. The other eight moods being elegant, majestic, repulsive, fierce, awe-inspiring, empathetic, and peaceful. On this aesthetic theory of the nine moods, see Thupten Jinpa and Jas Elsner, *Songs of Spiritual Experience* (Boston: Shambhala, 2000), 5.
69. See Gendun Chopel, *Grains of Gold*, 239.

70. Donald S. Lopez Jr., *The Madman's Middle Way* (Chicago: University of Chicago Press, 2005), 47. Rakra Tethong relates how this salutation to the Buddha came to be written. He says that one day Gendun Chopel told him, "Last evening when I was a little tipsy some of my companions kept asking me to compose a poem. So I wrote this verse. Later when I looked at it, I found it to be actually quite eloquent. So you should use this somewhere in the play about Emperor Songtsen that I have been encouraging you to write." See Rak ra bkras mthong, *Dge 'dun chos 'phel gyi lo rgyus*, 167. In fact, the poem would open Gendun Chopel's controversial work on Madhyamaka philosophy, *Adornment for Nāgārjuna's Thought*.
71. On Gendun Chopel's poetic style, see Lauren R. Hartley, "Heterodox Views and the New Orthodox Poems: Tibetan Writers in the Early and Mid-Twentieth Century" in, *Modern Tibetan Literature and Social Change*, ed. Lauren R. Hartley and Patricia Schiaffini-Vedani (Durham, NC: Duke University Press, 2008), 4–10.
72. See Stoddard, *Le mendiant de l'Amdo*, 330.